Form:uLA: Bryan Cantley

MECHUDZU

New Rhetorics for Architecture

SpringerWienNewYork

RIEAch Book Series
Editor: Guy Lafranchi

MECHUDZU
RIEAch (Research Institute for Experimental Architecture)
Berne, Switzerland, Europe

Printed in Austria

SpringerWienNewYork is a part of
Springer Science+Business Media
springer.at

Layout and Cover Design: H1reber, büro destruct, Berne, Switzerland, 2011

Proof Reading: Danko Szabó, Gräfelfing, Germany

Printing and binding: Holzhausen Druck GmbH
Vienna, Austria

Printed on acid-free and chlorine-free bleached paper
With numerous illustrations

SPIN: 80024747
Library of Congress Control Number: 2011932730

ISSN 1437-7446
ISBN 978-3-7091-0834-5 SpringerWienNewYork

Content

Author: Bryan Cantley
Co-author: Dr. Dora Epstein-Jones

THeoreti[cal]: TH o3 **4**
Essay – Drawing Strength from Machinery, Neil Spiller 4

Projects:
• Mobile Gatherspace 12
• Placemaker/Seedplanter 18
• The Batman Series 22
• i-P.O.D. 26
• Enantiomorphistic Inversions – Through the Looking-Glass Housing [The Alice Projects] 28
• Threshold/Knock Knock 32
• Wallmaker 34

GRaphi[cal]: GR o2 **40**
Essay – In a Galaxy Closer than We Think: Bryan Cantley's Marginal Architecture, Aaron Betsky 40
Essay – Drawing a ———— (The DNA of TnA), Dr. Dora Epstein-Jones 46

Projects:
• 3A Models 50
• Hybridrawings© 54
• Digital Paper® 64
• Greensheets/Topo:Typo 72
• NSFW Series 76

EConomi[cal]: EC o1 **84**
Essay – Machinogenesis, Wes Jones & Doug Jackson 84

Projects:
• Housing Prototype NH02 88
• X.Com 94
• TnA [Truth and Advertising] 98
• San Clemente CON-do RE:*surf*Face 102
• Santa Ana Monument Sign 104

ALchemi[cal]: AL o0 **106**
Essay – The Typo in the Topo, Bryan Cantley 106

Biography 116
Project Credits 117
Acknowledgments 118

o3TH THeoreti[cal]

When cities in the Orange Curtain finally ban cigarettes and plastic bags, there will be no more wafting ephemera in the way of the less physical ephemera that pervades this landscape.

American dreams.

Illusions of happiness.

Orange Curtains.

It is impossible to be here without a theory, for there is no here, here. Theory is the tether. It unites the landscape – into dream and despair, association and significance, buy and sell.

Mechudzu is a theory as practice – no hierarchies, no objects – a constant permutation of constant permutations, a means to a means.

This is the layer that resists the demand for wanting, but still retains the dynamic structure of desire.

Everything is theoretical. In the end.

Drawing Strength from Machinery

Neil Spiller

Twenty years ago Princeton Architectural Press published the very successful "Building Machines" issue of Pamphlet Architecture. It featured the mechanistic visions of Pfau/Jones, Neil Denari, and the gorgeously Dada works of Kaplan and Krueger. Real machines for living in inspired by hydraulic lines, JCBs, forklift trucks, aircraft, and all the metallic paraphernalia of late twentieth-century existence just before the computer became ubiquitous. It became an important benchmark in the "Architecture as Machine" idiom.

That was then and now is now – all things return but differently. During the last fifteen years, Los Angeles teacher and practitioner Bryan Cantley has added to this particular geneology of architecture and has produced a substantial body of work, which should be much better known than it is. Cantley's work with his practice Form:uLA is forward-thinking whilst obviously referencing the seminal work done before, but it is designed for a different world. A world where the computer reigns supreme and where machines and virtual machines are forever changing guises and functions.

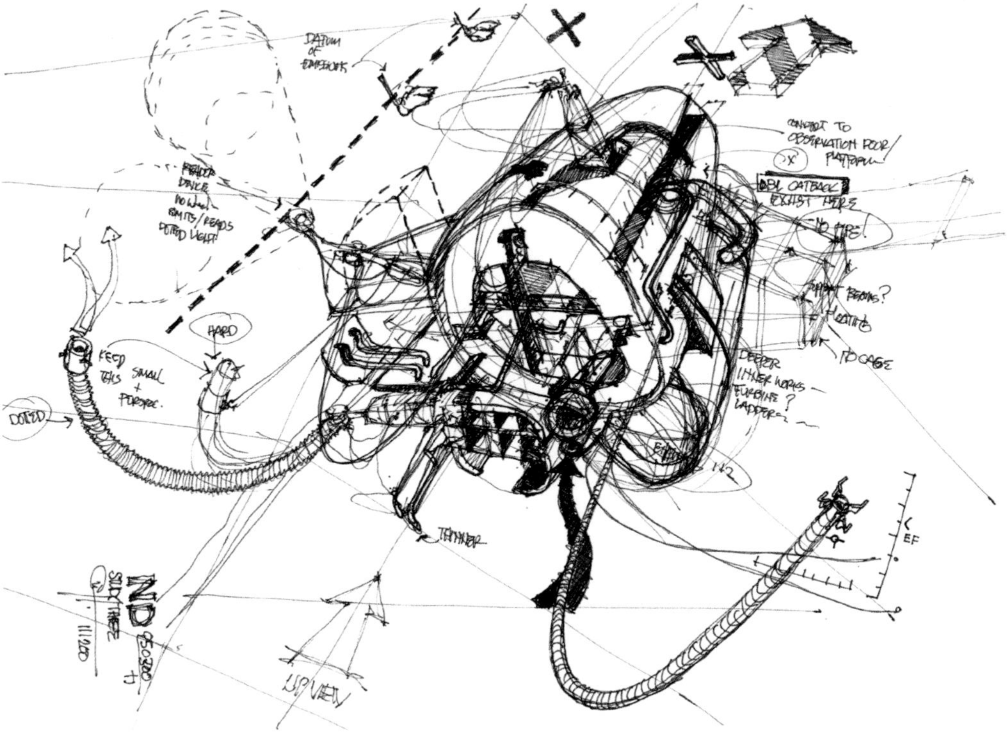

Contemporary existence involves navigating and operating a gamut of differing technologies and being conversant with a whole number of operational protocols. Imagine sitting on an aeroplane, whilst watching a video, a telephone in the armrest, an asthma inhaler in the pocket, a razor in the luggage, and a valentine's card rubbing against your laptop in its snug little bag. These simple everyday scenarios are the conceptual sites for FORM:uLA's architecture, which surfs, records, and posits in these fluxing machinic topologies and typologies. If you have a smart phone, and let's face it you probably do, you will be familiar with small "alerts" interrupting your surfing or emailing. When it does this the virtual machine of the phone, which usually pretends to be a word processor, a lap top, a camera, a gaming engine or a photo album, and a million things between, suddenly becomes a virtual geography teacher opening your mind up to a machine-augmented perception of a changing morphology of space and its fluctuating strata. This is cyborgian geography. This is our environmental context as much as any physical geography or transport infrastructure. There is a whole spectrum of morphologies based on the electromagnetic spectrum and a whole raft of cyborgian geomorphological archaeologists armed with many machines – some vintage, some state of the art – who can reveal their depths of spaces to us, as well as there fluctuating nature.

Architects have witnessed the growing fecundity of these types of spaces and have noted their destabilizing influence on the monopoly of traditional planned and designed space. However, few have speculated on what architecture might be or mean when partially immersed in these new digitized terrains. Bryan Cantley is one of these architects – who has sensed a need to develop new ideas, tactics, and strategies to save the architectural profession from navel-gazing itself into extinction. Why have architects lost their way? Architects are obsessed with form, they like the way their buildings look at the expense of everything else. Whilst this is not a crime in itself, it can leave them myopic to the great boon of the virtual – interconnectivity, expediency, and enabling of delight. Also, the global construction industry is fixed into series of simple economic relationships predicated on a very limited palette of materials, some of which have been around for millennia. The fast-evolving dynamics of software, hardware, and the flying freehold and leaseholds of the virtual world have yet to have any meaningful impact on the ubiquitous economics of the built environment, but it's coming to a node near you soon.

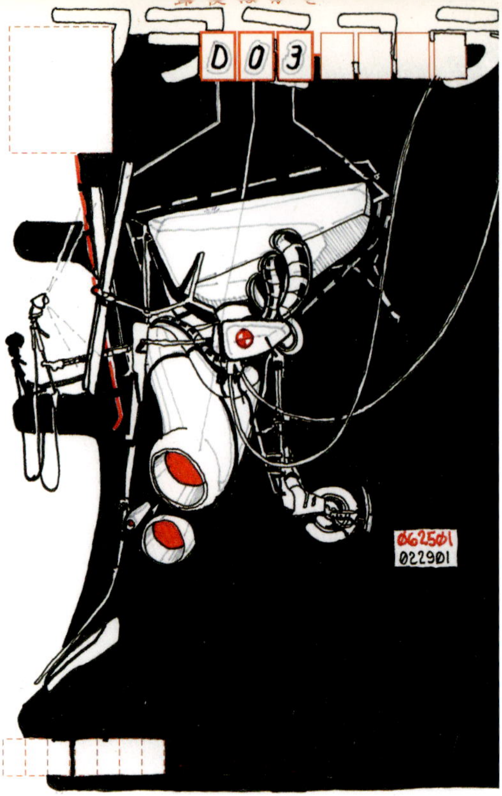

For Cantley, real sites are often the interstitial spaces of the contemporary city, its facades, and its datums. In turn, FORM:uLA's assemblies have a spatial fecundity of their own – that cossets and breeds spaces in tune with need, desire, and expediency. They are urban implants that mesh into roofscapes, sidewalks, and window reveals – forcing space and regenerating it. A FORM:uLA piece is a laboratory of form casting four-dimensional cartographies for possible new architectures. Formally the work has a kind of alien presence similar to a salon hairdryer out of control or behind the dashboard of a car or a mutant Airfix kit (An F111 meets Lawrence of Arabia's motorbike whilst on a trip to Japan). Similar to Neil Denari, whose father worked in aerospace, Cantley grew up on an American farm playing on tractors and other large farm machinery and experiencing a landscape calibrated by these metallic leviathans. Indeed, the pieces themselves still often retain the scale of the combine harvester. Yet also resonate with the notion of the "combine" in the art of Robert Rauschenberg – an architecture of ready-made, mass-produced objects, transferred images, subverted iconography, and emphasis on the viewer completing the work.

As FORM:uLA explains, their architecture has the "potential to exist in many places, or rather *any* place, at any given time. It is both site-less, and of many sites. It lies somewhere between the idea of mobility and multispatiality. Since the fabric of public open space often defines the urban setting, we saw this as an opportunity to allow critical need to determine architectural experimentation. Thus the idea of a docking station or site-specific system requirement at each site was also considered in the design of the project. We have been asked numerous times ' ... where the lines go that thrust off the edge of the page ...' This "docking scenario," or the notion of a place download, is one answer."

FORM:uLA and Bryan Cantley intrigue me; I should have seen this work earlier and so should you – buy this book, consume this book, bathe in its pixel juice. You haven't seen the last of this practice.

Neil Spiller is Professor of Architecture and Digital Theory and Dean, School of Architecture and Construction, University of Greenwich, London.

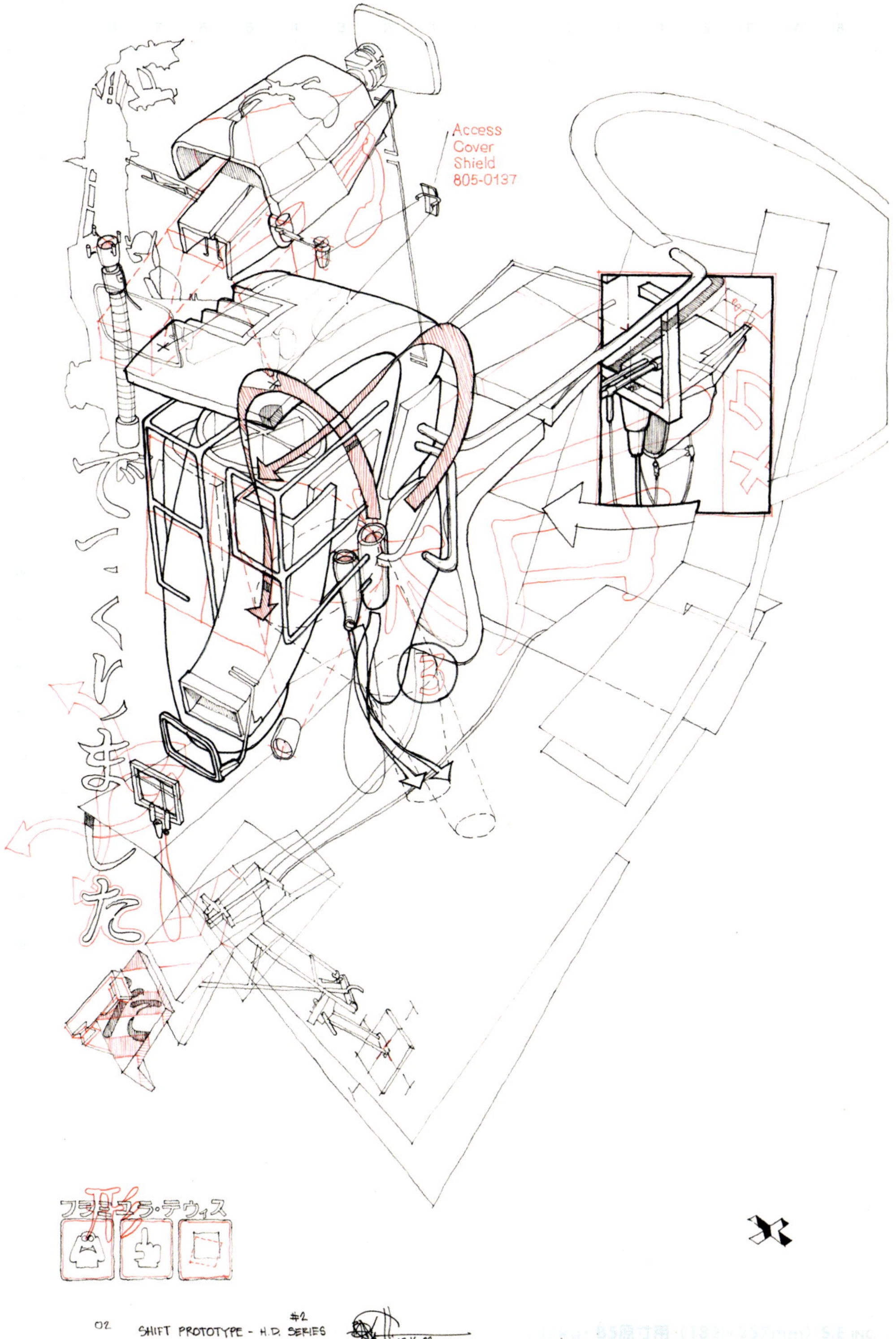
Access
Cover
Shield
805-0137
02
SHIFT PROTOTYPE - H.D. SERIES
#2
10.16.02

ALIGN
WITH
LOWER
RIGHT
CORNER
02

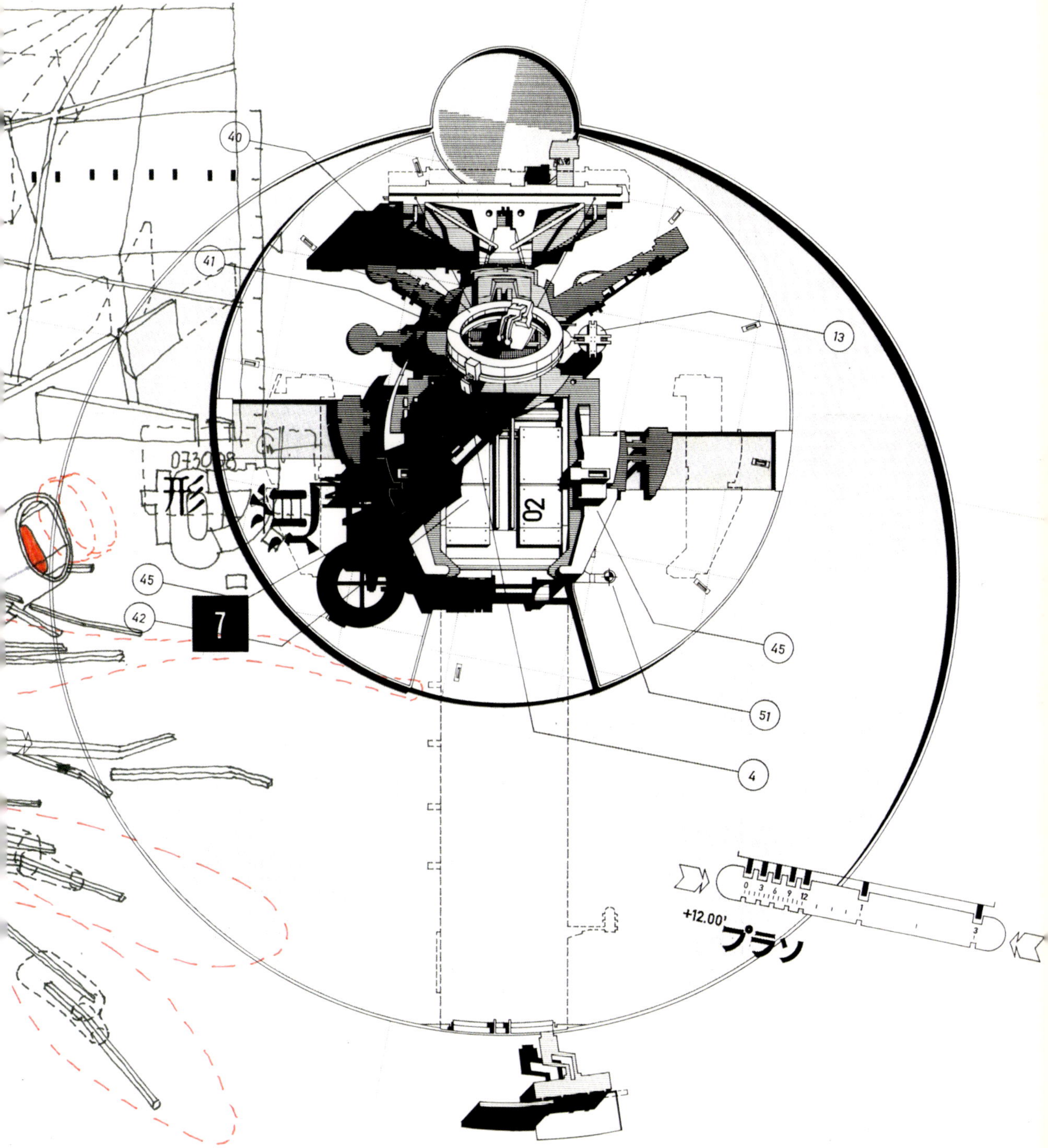

40
41
13
073098
形
02
45
7
42
45
51
4
0 3 6 9 12
+12.00'
プラン

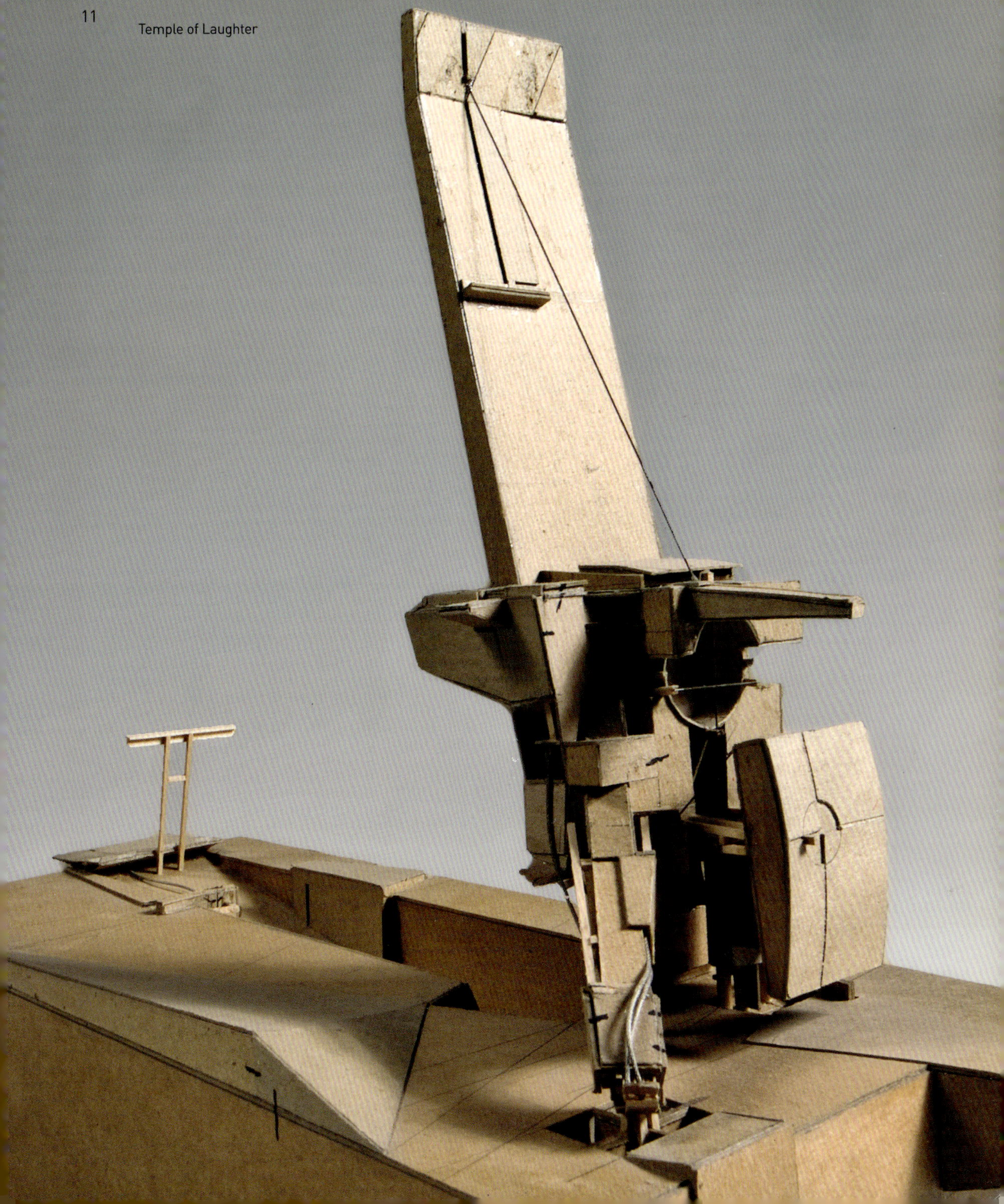

Mobile Gatherspace

The Mobile Gatherspace was explored as a floating civic plaza that travels from location to location, encountering various site and contextual conditions. It travels where needed, and leaves when immediate needs are quenched. In essence, it has the potential to exist in many places, or rather *any* place, at any *given* time. It is both site-less and of many sites. It lies somewhere between the idea of mobility and multispatiality. Since the urban setting is often defined by the fabric of public open space, this was seen as an opportunity to allow programmatic need to determine architectural experimentation and phenomenology. Thus the idea of a docking station or site-specific system requirement at each site was also considered in the design of the project.

A tension is produced by distorting and blurring the relationship of dock to vessel. The attempt is to pose the question to the observer of whether or not the dock is an anchor-like component, thrown out to provide direction and grounding, or whether the Gatherspace is simply mandated to dock at the preexisting outposts, with allotted program space. This paradox is an element of the augmentation of technology in architecture.

This is not a project of the current, of the *now*, but rather one that challenges urban and architectural thought of *when*. It is important to consider the future of architecture before we actually get there.

MGS – *terra firma* docking scenario. Actuator arms engaged. Stabilizer bars deployed. Hydraulic extension reel initiated. The public infestation begins ...
The new replantable landscape.

Worm's-eye view.

Access port deployed. Self-leveling *plazabanks* extended. Open bar seen at mid-level.

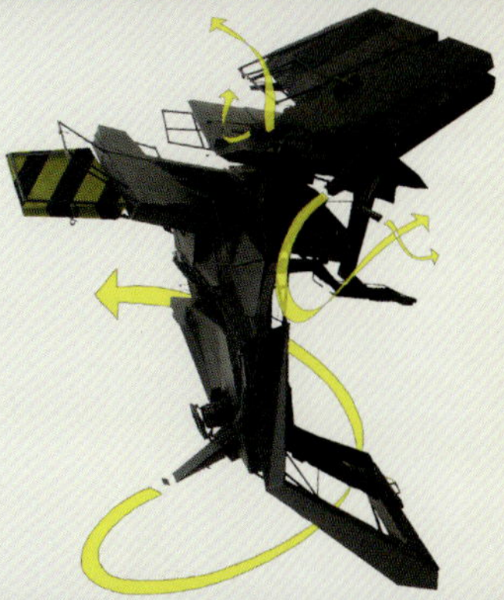

MGS – Context engagement. *Urbis* docking scenario. Multiple access points defined.

MGS – *terra firma* docking scenario.
Device in *full-blossom* mode.

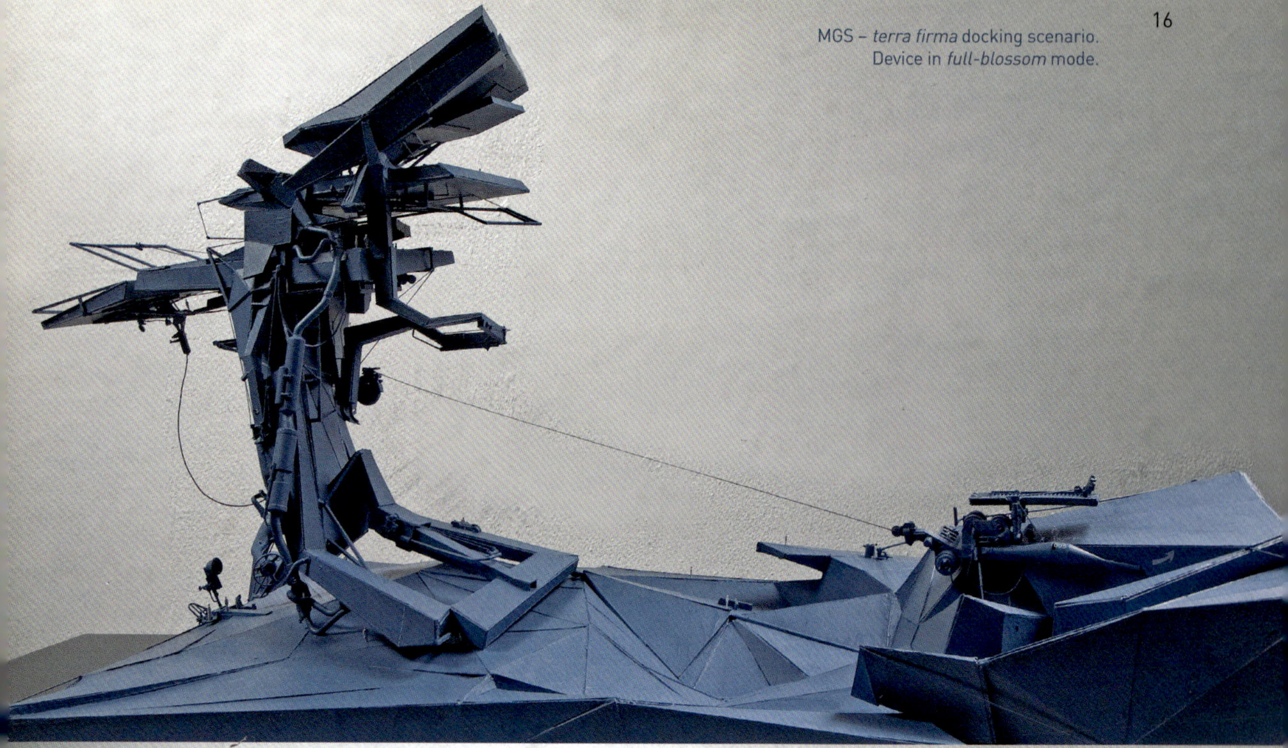

City engagement/political insertion commences.

Placemaker/ Seedplanter

This typology departs from the normal route we take in creating architecture. *Not a machine that is simply reflective of technology, but one that constructs it.* The Architecture creation machine ...

"... disruptive technology will bring with it disruptive social change ..." **WIRED.**
What is a disruptive technology? What is being disrupted – an existing physical structure; the fabric of a culture/society ... the facade of an existing building or a generic mesh ... comfort levels ... laziness factors?

What is the disruptive social change? A new physical structure ... or an "adapted one? Fragmentation/rebirth/reconstruction? A new social order? An embarrassed social order? An apathetic one? Is it a new weave," blended with the old, or a completely futuristic entity? A layered facade, showing signs of old and new? A not-so-generic, not-so-mesh [*anti-mesh*]? Higher comfort levels equaling higher apathy factors?

"... silico-, nano-, and bio- are the main denomination of value ..."
When will architectural manifestations begin to explore and express this future/soon-to-be-present culture? What is traded and consumed with this currency? How do you divide the "haves" and the "have-nots"? Is architecture an intellectual "property" that becomes the financial institution of the future culture? And what happens when the Luddites are forced into a financial exchange where they have no legal tender?

"... all cultural change is technology-driven ..." **William Gibson.**
Is technological change culturally driven? Is a specific culture ever in charge of its own technology? If so, then its own metamorphosis?

The Seedplanter is attached to a given generic architectural condition. It gathers data from the context; from the street; from the surrounding area; from inhabitants and passersby – and plugs the information back into itself. After processing occurs, *epigenetic* pods are planted/embedded on the site to develop into programmable architectural parasites. These may become inhabited spaces, service components, or

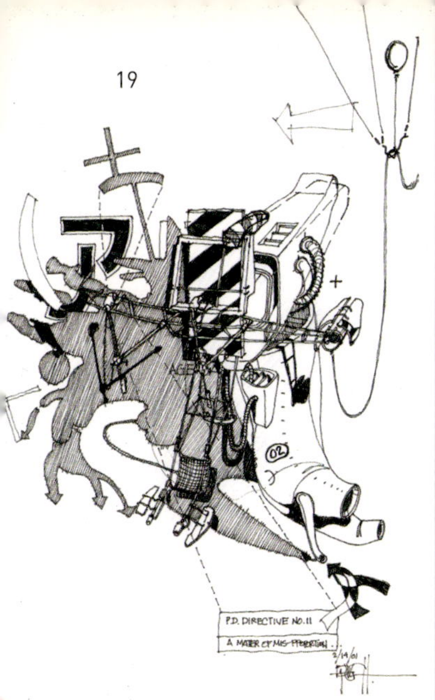

P/S in the process of data-harvesting in urban context.
The autobiographical architectural phenomenon.

facade "corrections"/augmentations, as the need arises. The concept suggests that the *pods* may erode and embed into the existing fabric or structure, employing the principles of **Mechudzu** as needed.

The Placemaker also deals with the ideas of replicating redundant and contradictory technology. The force of a turbo-charged hovercraft system is in conflict with the grace and simplicity of the air balloon support mechanism. The tubing and ducting that supply power to the unit as well as serve as data collection conduits are fighting the cable tiebacks to ask the question – is this itinerant or fixed?

This is only the planting device. It is not necessarily representative of the architectural language that may develop over time. The *pods* suggest no stylistic or formal movement. They are embryonic by their nature, with the vision of *seed* being as much actual as it is poetic. They are thought to be the ultimate elastic material, and will evolve without aesthetic bias. Perhaps there needs to be a Cultivator for the architectural improvement of the developed entity after component maturity. Can we "teach" architecture, can it be a learning organism, a smart entity?

The machine is "manned" – there is a main operator who must engage the system at an administrator level. Someone to initiate the sequence ... someone to flip the switch.

Someone to inhabit the process.

"Hi, there. I want to talk to you about ducts. Do your ducts seem old-fashioned? Out of date? Central Services' new duct designs are now available in hundreds of different colors to suit your individual taste." Brazil (1985)

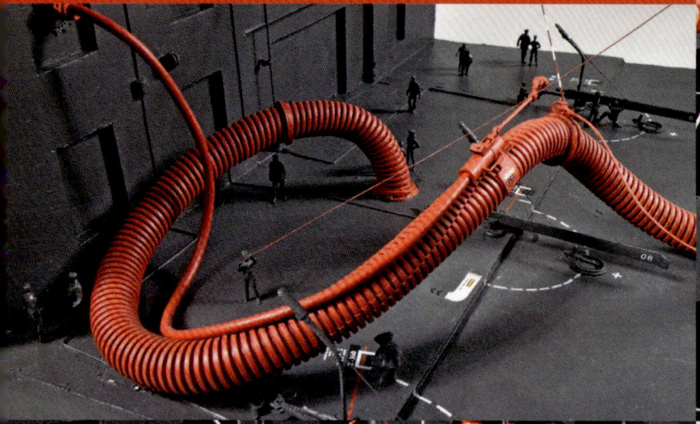

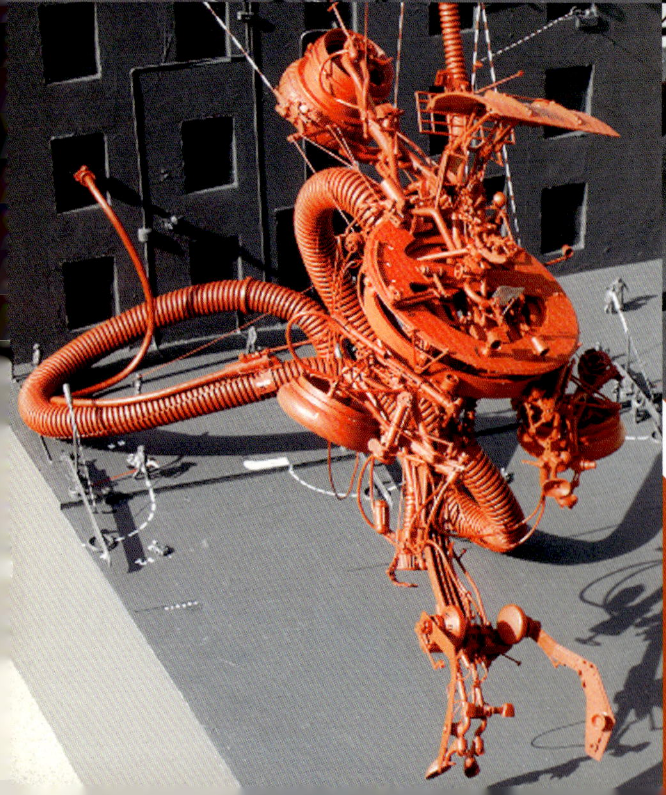

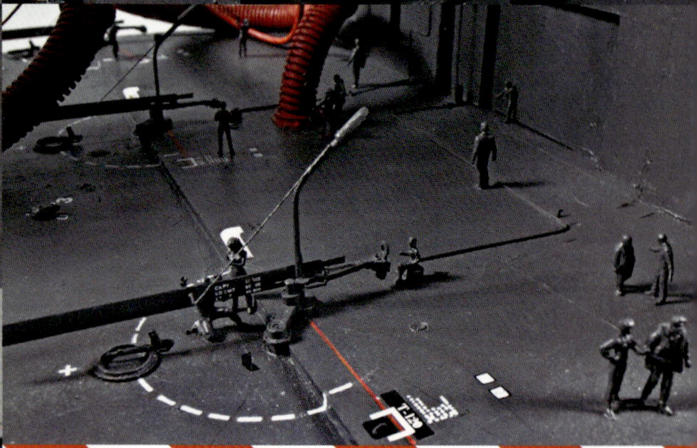

Exhaust manifold and Mechudzical sarcoma. System view of *on-line* jack-in points, serving multiple purposes of street lighting, solar charging stations (LEED), and waste-management robotic assistant hubs.

The Batman Series

"Batman": The Information of the Deformation.

The models are based on a set of 2.5-dimensional drawings that investigate hybrid dimensions, overlapping conditions, and multiple scales. By working in 2.5D, the models explore connections between 3D architecture and 2D graphic communication. Graphical data is derived from the original sketches and then used as a layering device to create three-dimensional entities. The form is therefore becoming a perpetual call-and-response between images and *3-[d]ata*.

There is an intentional overlap, blur, and fragmentation of traditional views of dimensional separation and definition. They are also examples of self-referential and self-critical architectural composites – architecture that exists to examine the formal nature of itself. They represent a revised object-space for architecture, one that is thought to open a dialogue for architecture that has been historically inaccessible.

The presentation of the series of models is imagined as a unification of case housings. Exterior graphic markings are derived from the original graphical exploration in an ICON format [read: ***ident-icon***].

"Architects Bryan Cantley and Kevin O'Donnell are interested in the examination of basic architectural elements, generated not by site or program, but as a purely investigative act. These sketches display a simultaneous series of basic compositional techniques – contrast of conflicting scales, interior/exterior relationships, multiple orientations, and overlapping conditions. Cantley and O'Donnell's Batman Models, also on view in this gallery, are devices in which the architects further "assemble, alter, reassemble, and redistribute original data found in the drawings."

Darrin Alfred, from Organic/Inorganic. SFMOMA, 2001

This model and drawing sequence are in the Permanent Collection
of the San Francisco Museum of Modern Art, Accessions Committee Fund purchase

カ

93
5
3

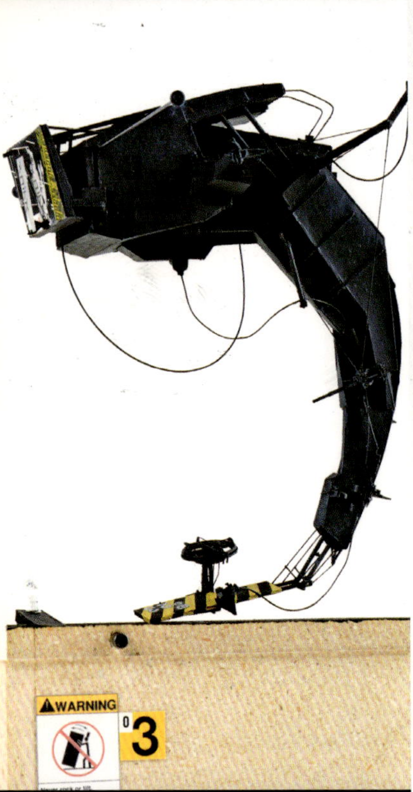

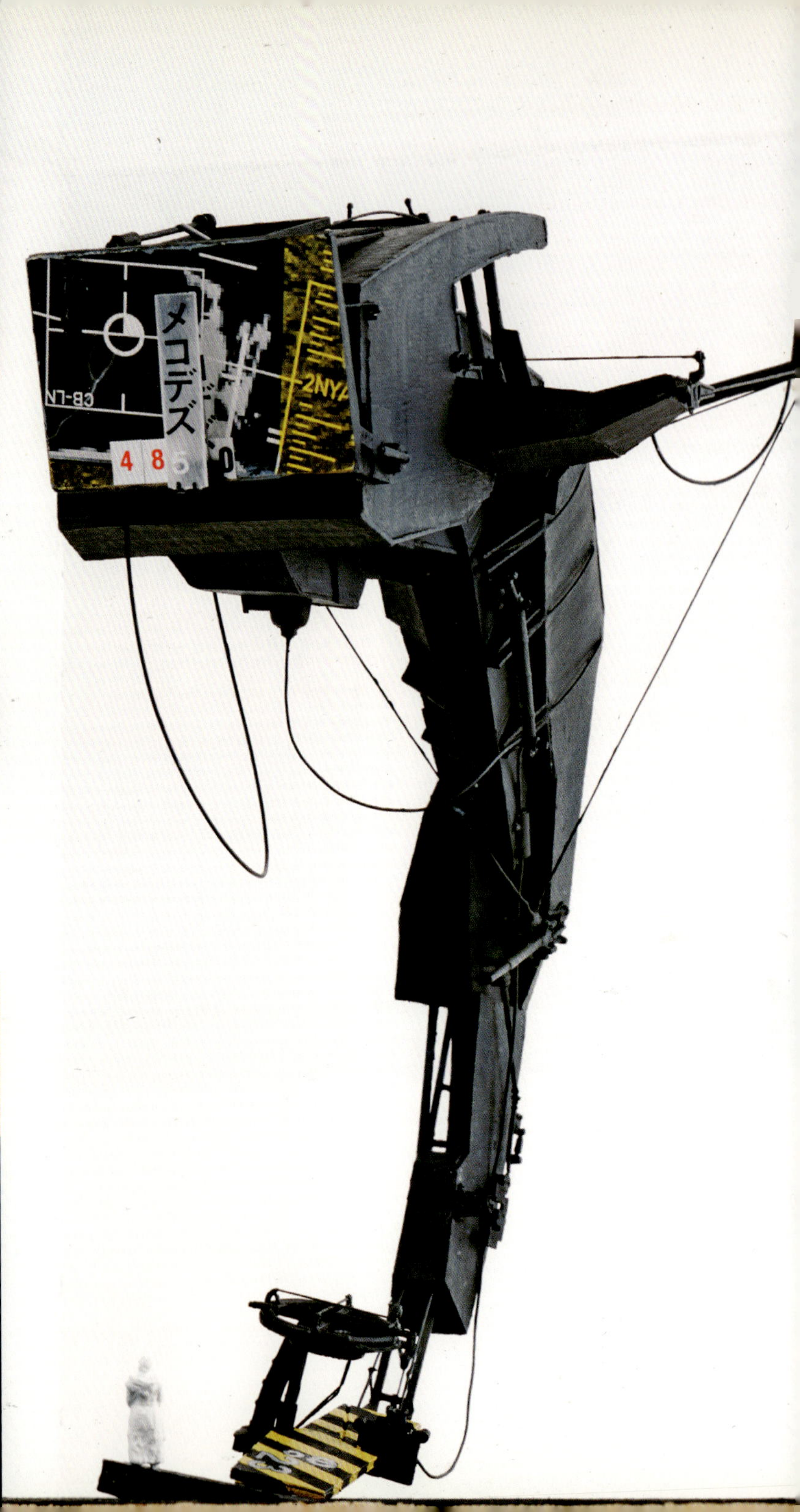

Machine-God to man? Human master
to nonthinking robotic slave?
Just who is driving this thing?

Temple of Architecture ... Church of the Machine.
Will you be an observer or occupant? Are you input or output? A new way to get "saved" ... Deletion? Wash away your sin[thetic] past.

i-P.O.D.

August 8, 2027 @ 3:27 PM, Orange County will achieve complete saturation density – maximum gridlock and absolute vehicular stagnation. Every available inch of freeway, on-ramp, off-ramp, surface street, intersection, driveway, drive-through, portico, parking lot, front lawn, and sidewalk will be filled with vehicular immobility. People will be forced to abandon their cars where they sit, and a new physical and social order will be born. There will be no release valve, no escape route. There will simply be nowhere to go.

The i-P.O.D. [Personal Occupancy Device] was a sampling of the competition entry for the "Changing Face of Orange County." We attempted to use the competition for a vehicle for the exploration of new architectural vocabularies responding to specific urban strategies; to use it as a discourse on what role architectural thought might play in future regional development; and to allow the combination of architecture and technology to bring about legitimate social change.

Quality of life became the project impetus, as it is affected by power and water shortages, longer commutes, greater disconnection between work and home life, alienation, and greater demands on personal attention that result from population increase.

The competition asked how to get one million new residents into Orange County by 2020. We answered by simply saying *"maybe we shouldn't..."*

The **Work/Live/Play** triangle manifest. Boundaries are blurred in the pre-mobile lifestyle hub. We were there long before the end of the *desktop* OS ...

The question becomes, in the removal of domestic waste and information: what happens to the binary that we flush away? Is it 0s and 1s, ...or just 2s?

Enantiomorphistic Inversions

– Through the Looking-Glass Housing [The Alice Projects]

Based on the book *Through the Looking Glass,* this project equivocates the physical landscape, the narrative landscape, and the landscape of the physical book.

The narrative landscape is one in which Alice must negotiate a checkerboard of brooks and hedges to progress to what she conceives as the end point. Alice's encounter with each brook invokes **horizontal** motion [the movement of the water – the x-axis], as well as the task of traversing the channel [the y-axis]. In addition, **the process of transformation** requires Alice to also pass through a **vertical membrane** to apply/affect/restructure the fabric [the z-axis]. After Alice passes over each brook, her environment morphs into a completely alternative situation.

The landscape of the physical book was also transformed, as we attempted to embody the conditions of a traditional book in the generation of the form. The project examines the state of the Enantiomorph – a set of entities that are mirror images of each other in structure, but have different internal characteristics and surfaces, such as Tweedledum and Tweedledee. The Enantiomorph is likened to Roland Barthes' *Death of the Author*, in that it reverses the role of authorship to one of the scriptor/reader, as well as the way in which a cover, page, text are distinct surfaces with radically variable meanings. An observer must be present to initiate the interaction but the mechanisms are interdependent – just as the satellite assembly needs the monitor to track movement. Alice depends on the Enantiomorph to wayfind across the x-y-z axes, but no architectural interface, no landscape, unfolds so logically.

Holo-cube and *Authorship Device*. If a book is read and there is no one around to write it, does it make a sound?

This building requires an operator and a user. Author and reader. The mechanical lung functions only when it loops, inhale/exhale.

The Authorship Device is read/write. It allows for the phenomena of observation and restructuration.

Rear Elevation. The *Holo-Cube* displays holographic interpretations of each chapter of the text.

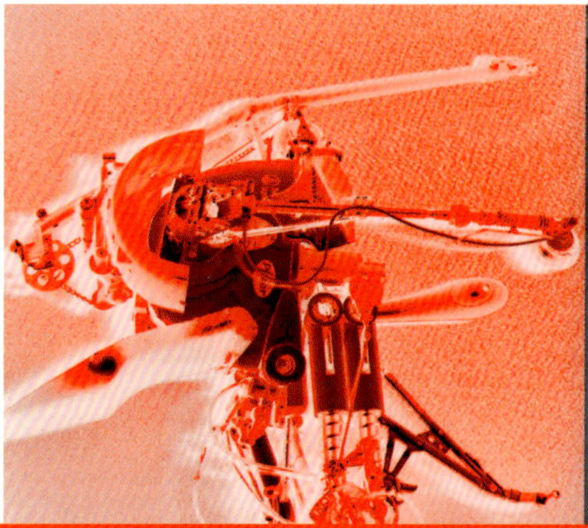

Threshold/ Knock Knock

It's a basic question, the one of the relationship to man and machine ... flesh and metal ... learned intelligence and *artificial* intelligence ...

This construct symbolically explores the threshold between worlds ... between souls. It proposes its own question, that of the *"who's there"*? [and perhaps just as important, "who's asking"?] ...

Is the machine set as the guardian into its realm, scanning and screening each potential *admin log in*? Does it seek to keep out viral intruders ... hackers ... humans who would dare upgrade [read: rewrite] its operating system?

Is it a sentinel who must collect user information ... saving the cookies of the human condition and location as pure data-food for its continued existence?

Or are humans the one holding the gate? Does the machine fancy life in a world of soul, of choice, of the flesh? Does it pine for feelings, the one type of data structure that cannot be consumed in its never-ending appetite to process? That seems pretty intelligent.

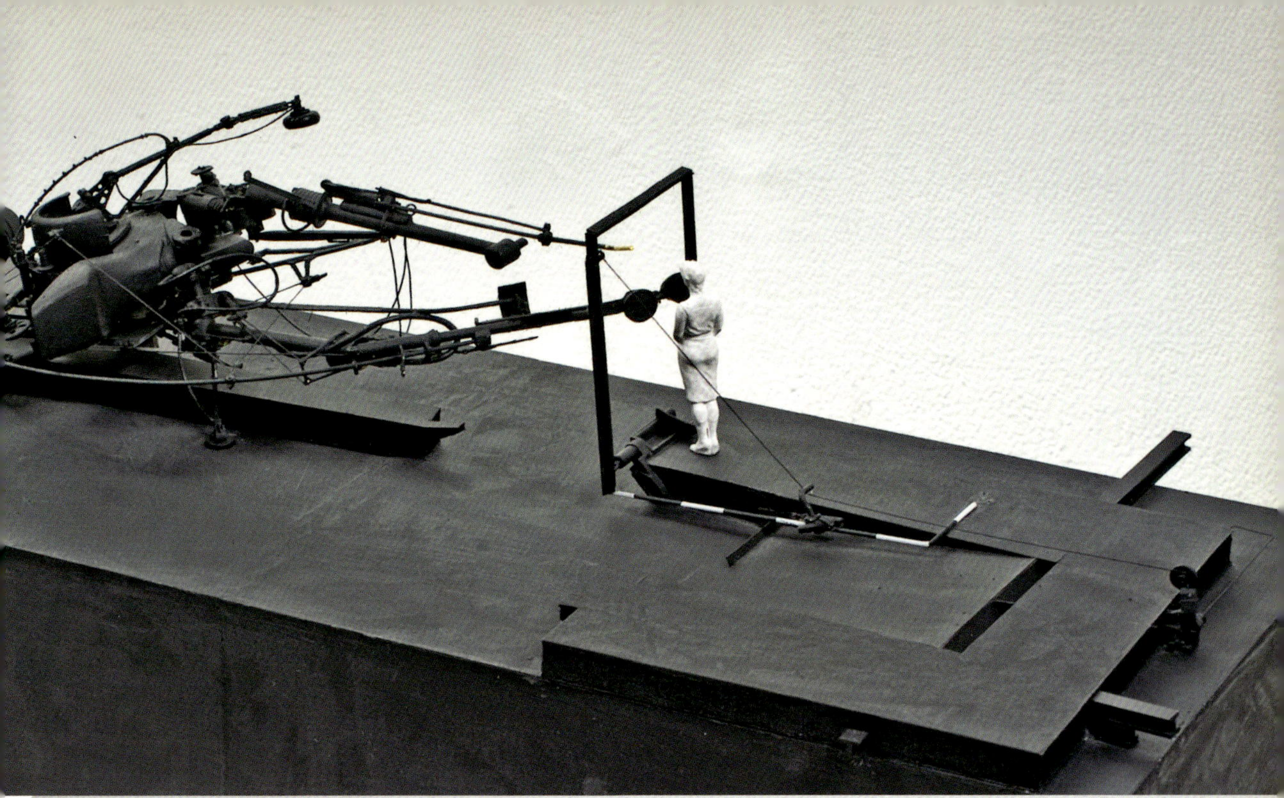

According to Arthur Koestler's theory, ghost structures can overpower higher logical functions, and are responsible for hate, anger, and other such destructive impulses. Dualism. Singularity.

Wallmaker

The Wallmaker is a prototype study for new collaborative drawing. We began to explore a series of architectural mechanisms that would, in essence, be devices that created their own context; their own need; their own time. Much as the drawing created itself [or its own platform], we envisioned the idea of an architectural entity that would do the same.

Each operation was thought of as a scenario that would create an architectural "standard" element, such as WALL, RAMP, WINDOW, etc., similar to the way in which the drawing created its own basic building component – the LINE. It maps out planar surfaces via laser-guided GPS systems. Intermediate framing is produced to give permanence to the laser/holographic outline. A rapidly manufactured wallboard or flexible substance is "sheeted" on top of the placeholder/frame.

"Interesting productive bias, it spits out walls and can be revealed by methods of making, rather than it being a tool for investigating and experiencing, which is my bias. I would like to do an exhibition about how the computer is changing the way things are made, rather than how they look, but that makes it difficult exactly as an exhibition ... It's like the Columbia reviews I was just on: there is no site, no user, no history, and no future, only the process of folding, splining, railing, or whatever Maya has spit out most recently ..."

Aaron Betsky, email dialogue on the Wallmaker.

"... The answer lies in how you define architecture. [I] contend that any spatial exploration is an act of architecture. Thus, the physical drawings, evidence of the mind's creative process, are not documents of architecture, but are architecture themselves ..."

Effie Patelos. Loudpaper. Volume 4, Issue 2, "Sub:line"

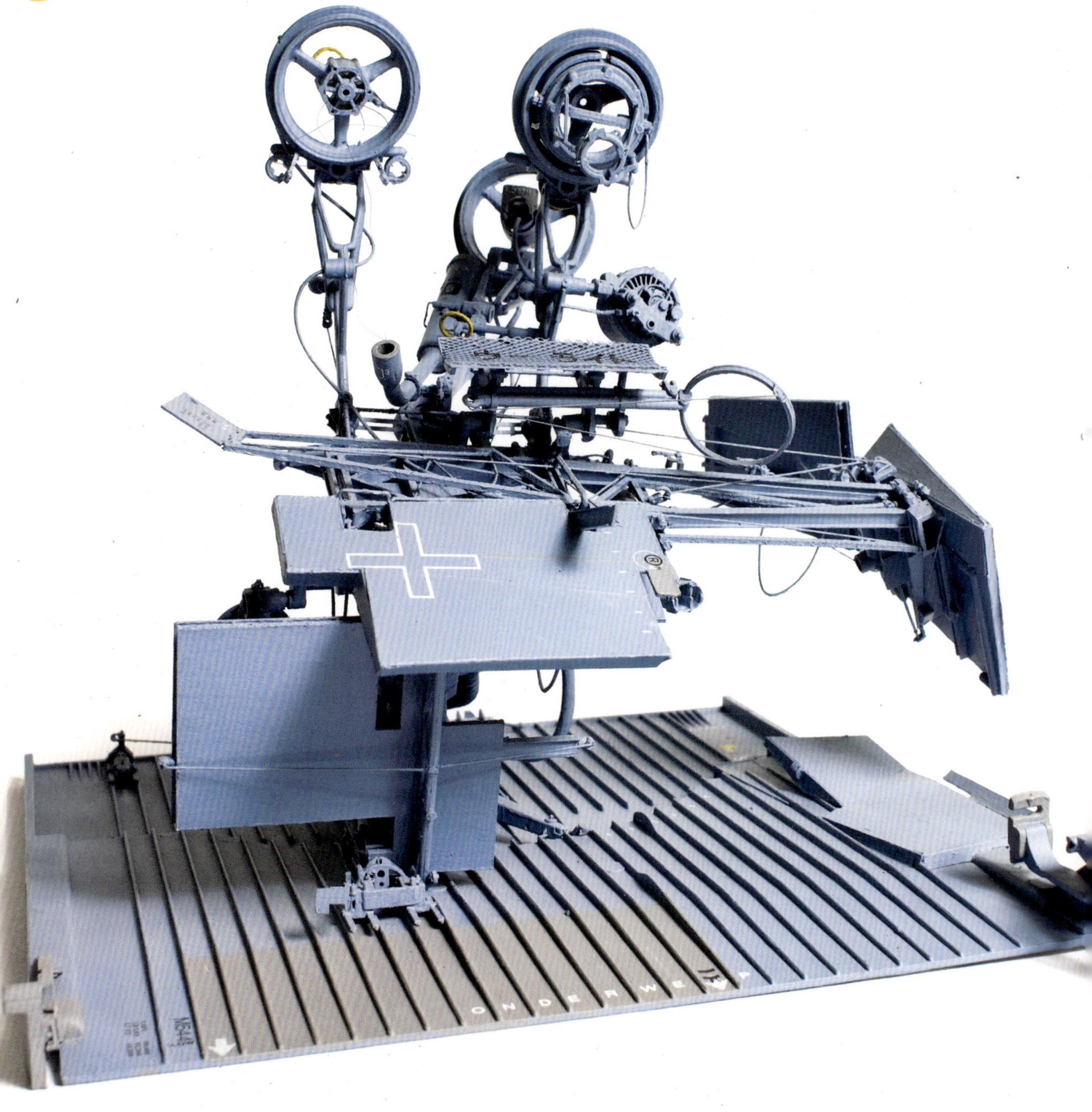

Study model of the *Onderwerp*. The self-constructing output device. An attempt at the visualization of the act of creation ... the Act of Architecture.

ABS

ライト

o2GR
GRaphi[cal]

Paper / paper.
Tablet / tablet.
Digital v. analog, analog v. digital.
("of course, that's not true ...")

This layer to the landscape is the one our eyes cannot help but read.

The topography of signs, of communicative devices – turn here, go, stop, buy big, get gas – weighs constantly for and against the type: typefaces, typologies.

("That restaurant looks like a bank!")

The graphical cannot be removed from the built layer – it forms the only deep roots known in the OC – old neon, McDonald's that still have arches – rooted also to the built layers to give them meaning.
It's not a meaning-meaning.

But that is what makes it interesting – Mechudzu in the vertical dimension. Fingers of signification – as fragile as a fleeting dot screen, as thin as brick veneer; but present, *presenced* in all that makes this visual climate visual.

In a Galaxy Closer than We Think: Bryan Cantley's Marginal Architecture

Aaron Betsky

Racing towards the future implied by the post-urban concatenation of human dwellings that is Southern California, Form:uLA envisions a world where the mechanical certainty with which we have shaped our physical environment dissolves into the endlessly hovering limbo of the freeway, the collage of the televised world view, and the directional certainty of diagrams that tell us where we are in nowhere. Bryan Cantley, the brain behind the post-architecture firm Form:uLA, gives us a chart to what he sees as our world. He is thus one of the last (though one hopes not *the* last) architecture visionaries looking beyond the needs of form and function to formulas for future orders.

The obvious inspirations for Cantley's work come from both within the traditions of architecture and from the world around them. It is worth tracing some of these histories in order to ground the free-floating imagery that flits across the digital paper. This context will not deny the work its originality, but points to the fact that its visionary quality, like all science fiction, is as much a dream of a lost world as it is a hope for or fear of a new reality.

Cantley's work floats. In its peculiar setting away from the world of construction that we might actually inhabit, floating somewhere in the place of imagination we grew up in in our media-saturated world, these forms do not provide the anchors of located power that buildings of note (what we think of architecture, or monumental form) used to furnish. Nor do they, however, open up free structures that let us imagine we can wander endlessly and in freedom. Instead, they exist like fragments of condensed technology, much like our cell phones, our cars, our various screens, and everything we use to navigate through our modern world. They are emblems of free-floating anxiety instead of kernels of either a dream or a nightmare.

Which is not to say that there is no certainty in these drawings. In fact, there is a surfeit of elements that tell us what is going on and where we are. Or so it would seem, for the arrows that would appear to indicate direction are as meaningless and disassociated from reality as the freeway signs pointing us to far-off destinations we will never reach on our way to a nearer exit, or like diagrams from a scientific journal illustrating flows that we otherwise cannot comprehend. For Cantley's arrows, sometimes straight and sometimes as waves or circles, do not lead anywhere we can reach or illustrate a direction we can comprehend. Instead, they are placeholders for some force that cannot be named or experienced.

Against this sense of force, Cantley opposes the thresholds on which we should, if this were a more classical composition, be standing as we gaze out into that strange new world. We know these are barriers or points of security because the architect calls them out in the black-and-yellow diagonal striping that warns us in our meat-world whenever we are nearing a precipice or just a dangerous step. The problem is that in this case the markings do not always denote an edge. At times they even become shape in and of themselves, enclosing a space. They do not just indicate a place of fear, but build that moment of possibly fearful transition into the body of the composition itself.

If these are the signs that float through Cantley's work, the body of his designs, such as they are, refuse to cohere. The most common element one can find in his work is a folded, angular shape that appears like a piece of bent metal. It is as if the hull of either a spacecraft or one of Neil Denari's mechanical buildings had been broken apart and Cantley were now elaborating this fragment. If there is anything we can still connect to solid forms we know, it would be the prow or three-dimensional bull-nose. This trope of late 20th-century architecture recalls the marine forms that have long been popular among modernist architects. It also has the advantage of being a shape that we cannot associate directly with one particular function, scale, or site, and thus is the architectural equivalent of the enigmatic, dense forms the abstract expressionist painters developed.

Related to the prows is the elongated and angular bar, usually made up of various segments. Perhaps the roots for this form lie in the "bar building," a modernist form that developed as a way to encapsulate what many architects saw as the linear movement inherent in modern life. First appearing in the quasi-visionary work of architects such as Moishe Ginsburg in Russia, it became a way of organizing "background" programs against which one could then play more formal elements housed in shaped constructions. Here, Cantley transforms the bar building into something that approaches an arm or cantilevered appendage, again turning what was background into a shaped element.

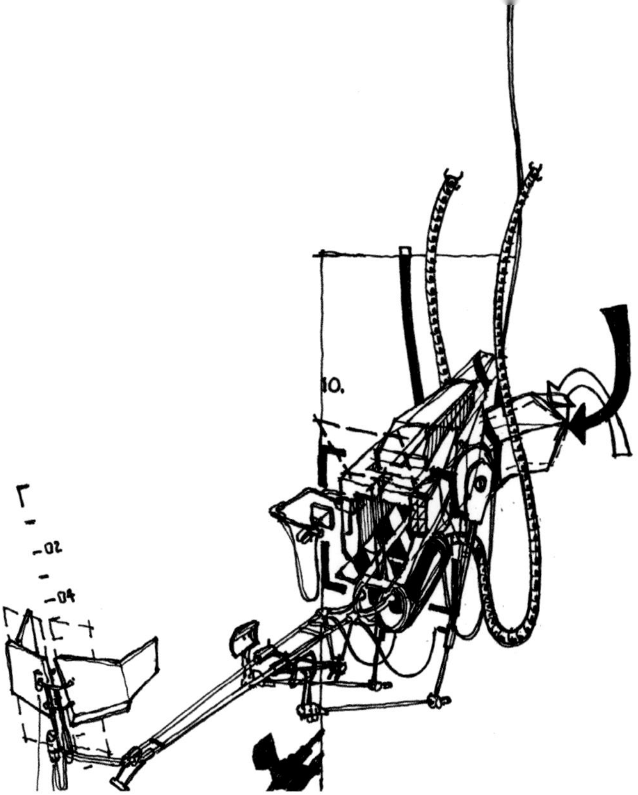

Beyond these more or less architectural elements, Cantley's drawings abound with more mechanical elements. There are what could be arms or legs, but are certainly some form of flexible extension, even if one does not know from or to what. There are cowl-like shapes and hoods, so that one goes looking for the body these fragments of armature might be covering. Such solid shapes do not exist here. There are Japanese characters floating through the space with the same clarity and weight as what could be buildings. It all just zooms past us, appearing to open in simultaneous windows and yet wondrously staying in balance in the one place where we can tell that there is a singular maker to this world, and that is in the finely honed sense of composition that makes Cantley's work simply beautiful.

Cantley did not invent all of these shapes or forms of composition, and acknowledges his debts to the architects and the films and comics that have inspired him. What he has done is to fragment them to an extent few other designers have dared to do, and to set them free in space while controlling them through design. This is partially the result of the place of the work. It is, quite literally, marginal: one of the drawings is a doodle in the corner of a printed agenda for an arts faculty meeting at the university where Cantley teaches. The work is also marginal in that it does not address or claim to address any of the issues that most architects see as central to the discipline. Instead, it is the free elaboration of elements remembered and imagined into incomplete compositions.

That sense of a radical lack of center is something Cantley emphasized when he started experimenting with "digital paper." Instead of pretending that the sketch is either something the hand makes based on what the eye does, or that it is a preparation for something to be built later, the digital sketch becomes a way of playing with line, plane, and form that is completely autonomous. In many drawings, Cantley reproduces the tentative and reiterative nature of the sketch by showing us the same form over and over again, slightly shifted, as if he were trying out various compositions. The difference is that in this case it is all these elements together that make the finished drawing. There is no before and after in these images, only the drawing out of the pieces themselves into something the maker thinks worthy of our consideration.

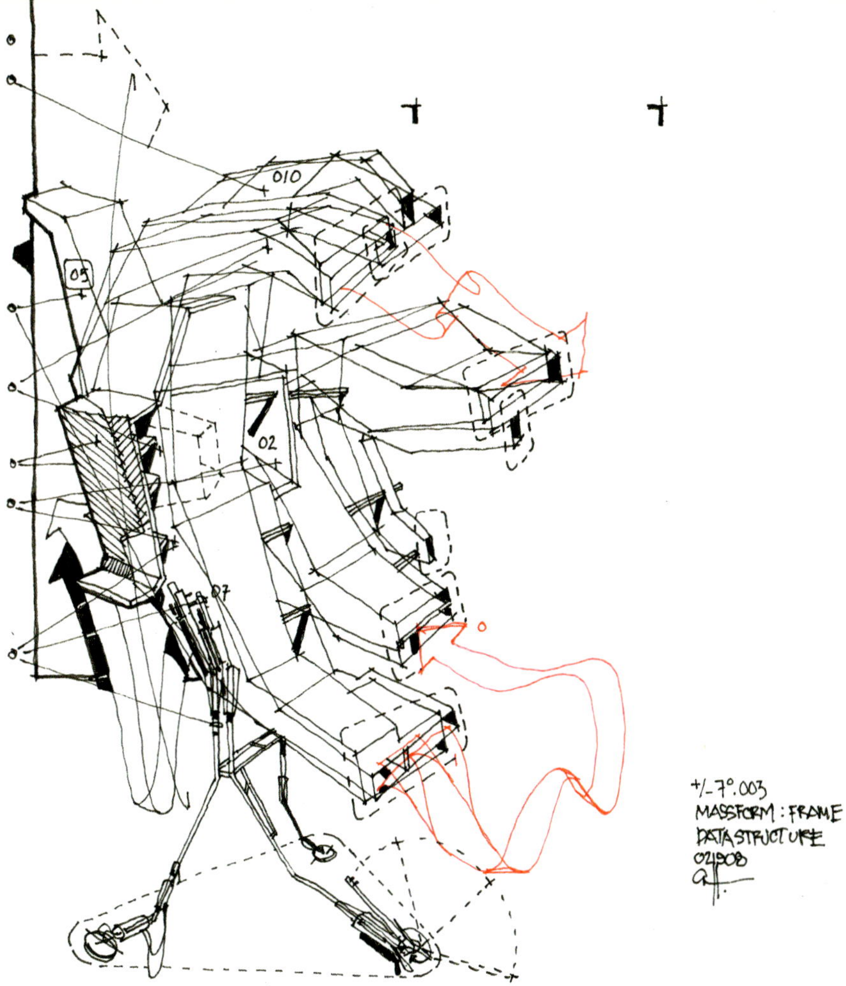

This sketchiness is part and parcel of the place Cantley has made for his work. He has described the work as "mechudzu," a kind of weed that grows wild on the body of our mechanical culture, luxuriating in its ability to draw energy from those forms, spreading quickly and choking off each single organism as it continues its sprawl. It would not be far-fetched to see in this mechudzu an analogy to sprawl and its smoothing of the mechanical world into a seamless ooze of human habitation in which all edges are blurred, all forms and constructions are hidden, and conditioned space spreads out over the planet. Mechudzu is a critical palimpsest for sprawl, bringing out the fragmented yet continuous forms that lie hidden inside its tract homes, freeways, and shopping malls.

In one of his drawings, Cantley shows us a new Adam and Eve at the core of his marginal universe. He took these figures from the attempts by NASA to communicate who and what we are to civilizations in other galaxies. This naked man and woman are surrounded in this version by a rotating family of mechanical forms, barely held together by the fragments of architecture the designer has mixed into this eddy of black lines. This is an "exploded diagram" that we encounter most often when we are trying to put a piece of equipment together. In this case, it is not showing us how to assemble anything. It does not even make sense as a singular object. Instead, Cantley presents us with the fragments of our world. He leaves it for us to make sense of them, to hang an ideology on his composition, or to decide whether we are looking at the ruins of our civilization or the building blocks for the next one. He only doodles and draws, working in the margins to present possible moments of coherence inherent in a world of sprawl.

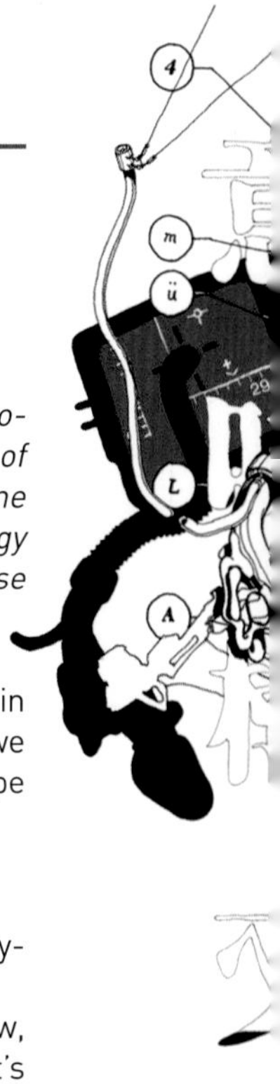

Drawing a ——————
(The DNA of TnA)

Dora Epstein-Jones with Bryan Cantley

BC: *"The interjection and superimposition of the flesh and hand back into the fluidity of the design process has had a great impact in our problem-solving. The ability to draw fluidly in 3D affected the DNA of all design processes and decisions, and, ultimately, the construction process. Spaces and forms became hyper-fluid in their development, as initial gestures and alterations worked with traditional methodology of hand and pen, flesh and machine, without the layer of interference and disembodiment that the mouse and keyboard offer."*

There is a moment in Bryan Cantley's TnA project in which what might be termed the "ceiling" folds back in on itself. It's a little moment. A quick reveal. A peekaboo. Under the "cladding," "the ceiling envelope," we see the other ceiling, ponderous and dark, the old machine – what has been. Below the fold, the envelope settles into the wall, holds itself up, or appears to do so at least tectonically – what will be.

A single moment.

It's unbearable.

It "reads" like architecture. It is architecture, certainly. There's structure and skin, volume and space, layers of architectural stuff. It's got to be architecture.

And yet, it is both distant and immediate, tectonically nonsensical – the rhythm of the fold is off, somehow, canted to the acute angle and still floppy – and tectonically imaginative – hey, who says it can't do that? It's deep too. Not just layers but dimensioned in all dimensions.

And to this puzzle, Cantley offers an explanation through a process that is just as confusing, just as familiar and defamiliar. Drawing in 3D, drawing and the computer, drawing in the computer, flesh and machine ... Drawing a ————.

There are no direct words for this activity, for this relation between drawing and building. It defies all previous categories or ontologies. This is NOT (it should be noted) a postmodern blurring, a "both/and" that ultimately challenges the hegemony of authorship. Authorship is alive and present – and it is in reality (stress the reality part here) not both/and but neither.

This ———— is a different architectural creature altogether.

TnA, and its delightful confusions, can be traced directly to a device that Cantley calls "Digital Paper." Digital Paper is one way that Cantley has devised of using pen tablet computers as a "disruptive technology," an evolutionary step along the tradition of hand-pen-paper drawing. Digital Paper uses the graphic software's layering abilities to create a conscious simultaneity – what he calls "live active layering." He practices in a "freehand" manner, but he calls upon a Cartesian "fourth dimension" in order to manifest multioriented spaces and spatial orientation. TnA is hardly simple, even if it is fundamental – the same is true for Digital Paper.

Digital Paper is naturally, artificially, a reconciliation. In the early days of the computer's introduction into architecture, and even through today, there has been a marked belief in the difference between the computer and the hand. The hand, as observed most beautifully by Mark Wigley, is the instrument of a genius god, the light of inspiration flowing down from heaven and into the nimble fingers of the architect, the lovely breath

and sigh of the quick sketch, or the intentional hand to more mechanical drawing set. The computer, (punningly), on the other hand, is the instrument of removal – the hand to the mouse, the mouse to the computer, the computer to the screen, and so on – even to the point of advanced animation softwares that promise to remove the author altogether. Cantley, in using the Digital Paper, the Tablet, sees it quite differently,

BC: *"The distinction of 'digital' versus 'analog' can refer to the method of input, data storage and transfer, the internal working of an instrument, and the kind of display. Ironically enough for the intent of this narrative, the word 'digital' comes from the same source as the word digit,' namely, digitus: the Latin word for finger – (counting on the fingers) as these are used for discrete counting."*

For Cantley, then, the "digital," from "digit," stands for the presence, not the absence, of the hand. In the early days of animation software applications in architecture, there was an intended critical move away from authorship. The computer, it was reasoned, could process architectural envisioning on its own – once the booleans or parameters were set, the machine would work away, digesting, changing, ultimately authoring the design outcomes. The beauty of this nonauthorship was also the potential novelty for new forms. The computer was thus also seen as a chaos machine, capable of exotic and unanticipated formal transformations. And so, what had started with a more critical move (perhaps traceable to the more analog "diagram") became an entirely new rhetoric of the postcritical – nonauthorship, novelty, transformation, Deleuzian becoming.

Digital Paper is emphatically authored, but it is no less capable of producing all of the furrows and folds, layers and illegibles that are usually assigned to the Rhino/Grasshopper/Zoo Fauna of software. In this way, Digital Paper is more like the classroom doodle – the wandering mind and the loose hand creating enormous and complex layers of compositional disrespect.

Cantley describes the basic components as if it were a drawing class, but at every turn, the chaos takes over – the sense of control believed to be nurtured in the act of drawing frays, deforms – to be exact, Cantley says it "informs," in the sense of formal exploration using digital (hand/mouse/cpu) data. Here, a description of the six Digital Paper methodologies begins instrumentally and continuously unravels:

BC:
1) Ground[s]: the implied layers of a drawing or visual field. This is where perspectival points are established and reference points exist. They inherently contain the "secondary" data, such as construction and projection lines, radii designations, grid constructs, and the like, including the information about the construction of the drawing that is often overlooked or erased.

New typological relationships between layers and overlapping of traditional "grounds" [backGROUND, midGROUND, + foreGROUND develop, mutate, and evolve into new unknown conditions.

2) Layering: the digital manipulation of images on top of other images, with the ability to apply distortion filters for the purpose of examining new relationships between two or more layers that overlap.

3) Color/fill: the filling of selected shapes or areas with available patterns or solid colors. The ability to quickly apply pattern fills into a true sketch allows for an increased level of field experimentation. Fill recon-

ceptualizes the drawing as a process rather than a product. Fill is typically applied to the finished product, as it is exceedingly difficult to experiment with large areas of fill by hand. It's unfeasible to completely erase ink and color blocks from a drawing without leaving some trace.

4) X/Y Dimension: defined as the thickness or thinness of a given pen stroke. The ability to quickly change digital pen widths, from razor-thin to paintbrush-thick; or to an automatic dotted or dashed line, decreases production time while, most importantly, enabling the author to think graphically and dimensionally within the event of the drawing itself.

5) Erasure: defined as the removal of a drawn entity ... the act of "noncommitment" ... the nonline ... the act of "with-drawing" ...Tablet computers allow the user or author to actively edit the work, in real time. With traditional input-media, the authors have control only over additive processes – drawing lines, generating shape, committing registration permanently to paper or receptacle. In the digital pad environment, they have the ability to operate in both additive and subtractive modes. It has taken technology, or an aversion to high technology, one might argue, to make us truly aware of the power of a very low-tech entity such as the eraser.

Drawing with an eraser is the anti-line. If one moves past the surface structure of this condition, the potentials of the anti-line become quite varied, and will produce alternative paradigms in drawing and designing.

6) Direct Translation: the condition in which the digital entity is the first true generation, opposed to those considered second generation, such as copy or scan. The tablet is not thought to be a translation device, it is in fact a digital entity. It seeds without loss of resolution, without color misinterpretations, without resolution mishaps. To put it simply: it is what it is.

Working through each of the above methods, each is also indexed as a methodology – that is, for every action on the tablet, there is a corresponding orientation to the process of drawing. This is not merely faster communication or processing speed, it is an intentional and conscious exploitation of instantaneous switches, changes, and differences ultimately aimed at a new way of imagining the process from concept to building.

Digital Paper would not be possible without the tablet PC, or generous funding for Cantley's innovative and daring use of it. And to this end, he cleverly "trademarks" it, signaling his own imbrication in the culture of privacy that pervades his home county. Orange County's seemingly endless sprawl has been typically read as a surface – a single layer, superficial, but there is a powerful commentary in even that through the way in which he draws. Indeed, the OC is layered, and all of the layers, whether compatible or not, in-form: the graphic layers, the physical ones, the economical and the political.

Cantley enjoys the layers, the way in which they conflict – how one might "vanish" and how others magically appear. It is layering that the tablet does so well – there is never a need to translate a drawing through multiple scans to produce layers. Instead, even "low-tech" software like Photoshop allow for the possibility that the layers themselves are a design advantage, that the existence of the layers and the tablet's unique ability to act as a kind of "depth finder" create conditions not only for new types of drawings but also for a radical resynthesis of the entire design-to-build process.

BC: *The removal or synthesizing of these segregated layers of chronology and task promote a much more fluid and experimental approach to design methodology. When the tool becomes simple, the access to the design intent, and not the operation of the tool, becomes the focus.*

TnA is beautifully situated – an advertising agency (graphic information) in Santa Ana, California (Orange County dreg city) – an interior remodel of existing office dreck. As a project, it should not have called for anything other than some warmer, softer wood-slatted walls and a little ceiling kookiness to create an architectural impression. Instead, Cantley used the simultaneity of the Digital Paper – in this case, mostly SketchUp as the software choice – to prove that the layered approach is not merely instantaneous but capable of producing new, innovative spatial conditions in real time. As an architect, Cantley could have discussions with the client, produce on-the-spot drawings, even prepare construction documents, all within the space of a meeting time. The corporate fantasy is satisfied in this mode, especially an OC-corporate fantasy – but more than that, the effect of this simultaneity, this live action layering, is the very effect of the architecture itself.

TnA is therefore not a product in that its multiple readings are not intentioned as an outcome. It is more a point in a process where multilayered applications of media are rendered. TnA doesn't start first as a sketch on paper and then a computer model and then a set of plans and sections and then a construction set. Instead, it is the paper – the folded and chamfered plates of the project attest to this immediate connection – it is the medium of the experiment. For Cantley, the physical is just another layer in the tablet – so when we see the layers of TnA, we are in fact seeing the darkness within the drawings that made the voids, the angles that establish the space. This is the source of TnA's defamiliarization route. The black blackness of the pen may be deep in the physical as it is in the graphical or it may be the shadowed surface of the wall. It's still a wall, but remember, a wall is still a surface.

Ultimately, what is truly promising about this work is that it entirely undoes the established relationships between drawing and building architecture, but in no way does it ever reject architecture. It is emphatically architectural. And in so being, it brushes against the delightful to watch his critics flounder – to see them squirm as they try to describe what they see. It is the job of the critic to see – to make legible, to make relevant, to relate – and yet, Cantley's TnA keeps slipping away. It feels like architecture – as in, that must be an axon, I think that's a plan, I'm certain that this part here is a wall.

The work of Bryan Cantley is especially indicative of the experimental potential of drawing. He is certainly not content-shy – there's a kanji character, there's an arrow, that must be an actuator, I think that's a hose. But, he determinedly takes all forms equally – from their 2D presence on the paper into the realm of the layer, and from the layer into the realm of the third dimension. Each drawing on the Digital Paper is really more than a drawing – and yet not a model as it does not represent anything to be built later. It is built as it is present – stacked, collided, folded. So, when an encounter is made with the physically built work of Form:ULA, the effect is exactly similar. The drawing is a building. The building is drawn.

In real time. The hand is present, continuously, fluidly.

Fill in the blank.

3A Models

These were a short series of experimental spatial constructs, or models, reconciling the notion of architecture as an almost wearable condition of skin, cloaking, and expression.

In general, models have the ability to tell us more factual information than drawings, simply by the fact that they are dealing with a miniaturization of realspace, or tangible evidence of matter. Modeling gives us the opportunity, when using it as an extension of drawing, to examine the paradoxes that are established in the lies of drawings. These untruths allow for spatial interpretations that would not have existed without the falsehoods of the two-dimensional.

Models also provide a rich laboratory for harvesting receptacle surfaces – conditions that may impregnated with drawing media as part of the exploration. Whereas drawing on a model may not be a new idea, the opportunity to read demarcations on modeling surfaces as data, and especially as data that may influence the design process, is a strong consideration in our studio.

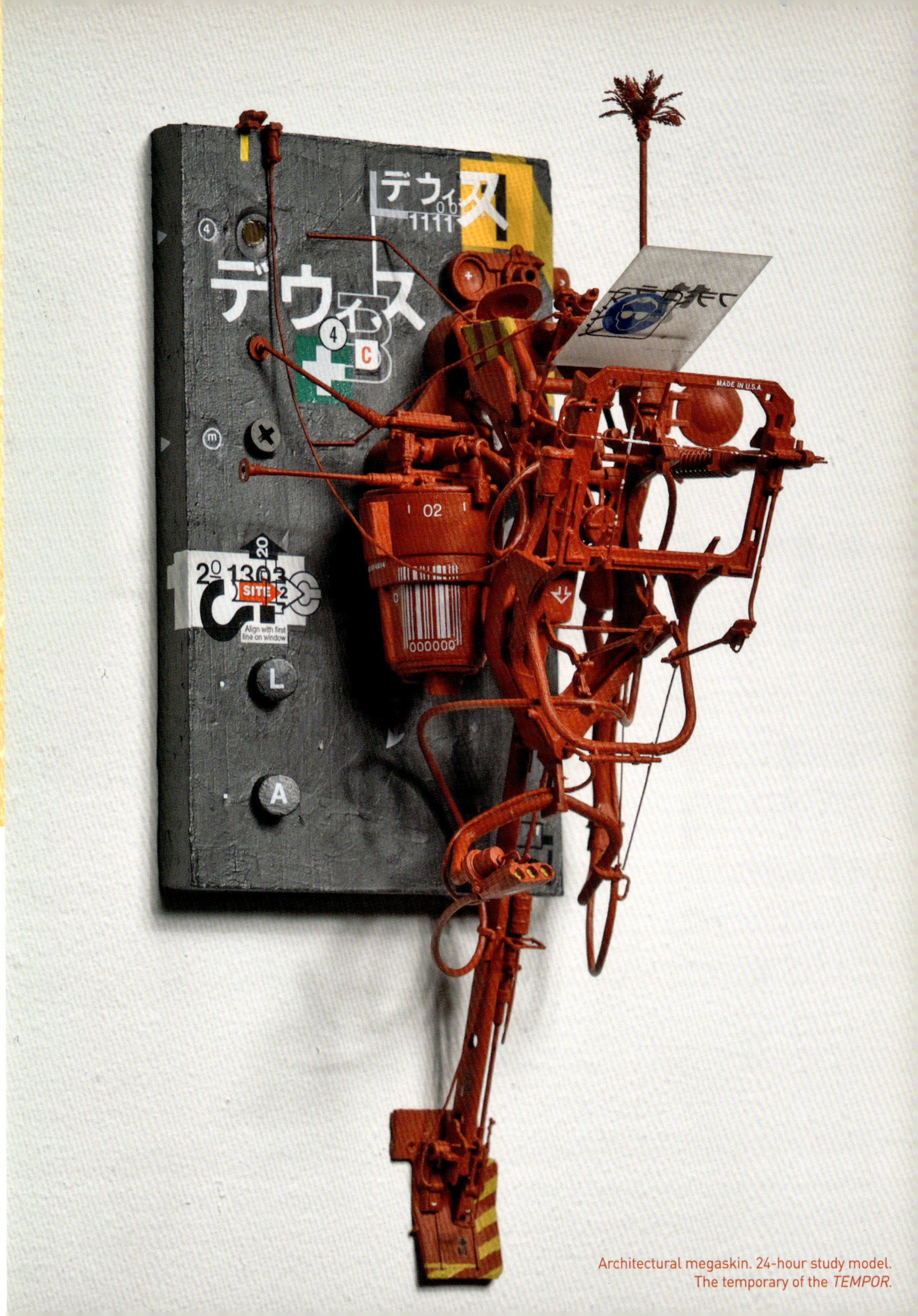

Architectural megaskin. 24-hour study model.
The temporary of the *TEMPOR*.

Each of the four was built in exactly 24 hours.

As we attach to the innards of the host, so does it attach to the innards of its context. Skinning the liebes.

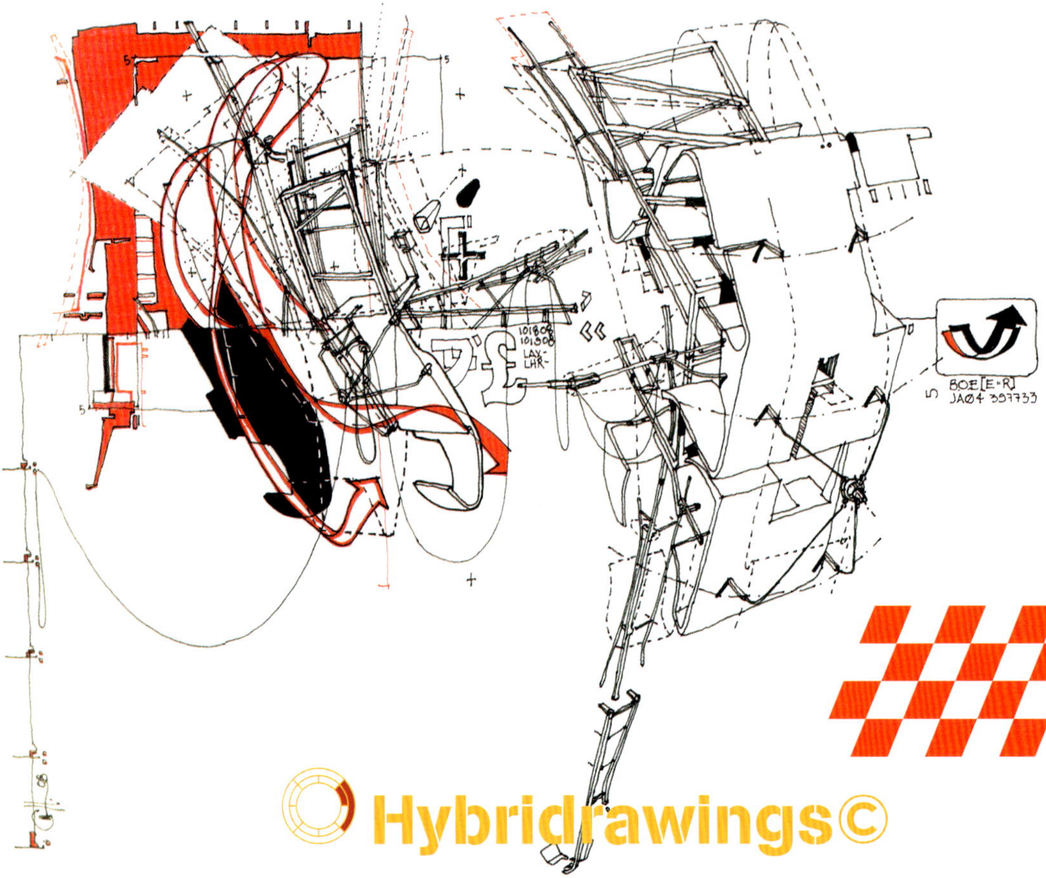

Hybridrawings©

Hybridrawings are representative of an ongoing experiment in harvesting 3D architectural *form-space* within the edifice of 2D communication. They purposely fragment and reconstruct traditional views of dimensional separation and definition.

They are based, in part, on studies of the 4th dimension referenced in from digital and hyperspace theory – that *entities may occupy the same SPACETIME* without disruption to either component. They investigate digital imaging software, where *layering* has emerged as a design methodology. It is within these overlaps and simultaneous existences that we are able to conjure a new architectural *form-space*.

"...The motif of Form:uLA's design language is always the machine – the man-made in its most generic form. At first glance their drawings look like overly fussy mechanical diagrams, the kind you might see in Victorian-era equipment catalogs. But look more closely, and the drawings' hybrid parts refuse to compose ...The assembled whole is defiantly abstract: the more you try to read the drawing, the more agitated the unresolved elements become. The overall effect is disorientation, and that is the point.

The drawing is clearly not, as architectural protocol would dictate, a set of building instructions or a depiction of a particular space. It does not obey the architectural mandate to construct a more perfectly ordered world. Instead, it is an invitation to abandon order. The drawing itself is Form:uLA's laboratory, a fluid, boundaryless, unpredictable environment in which every idea the two architects have – deliberate or accidental, serious or ridiculous, revolutionary or merely subversive – is let loose to metastasize ..."

Ruth Keffer, Loudpaper. Volume 4, Issue 3

NC 17
466

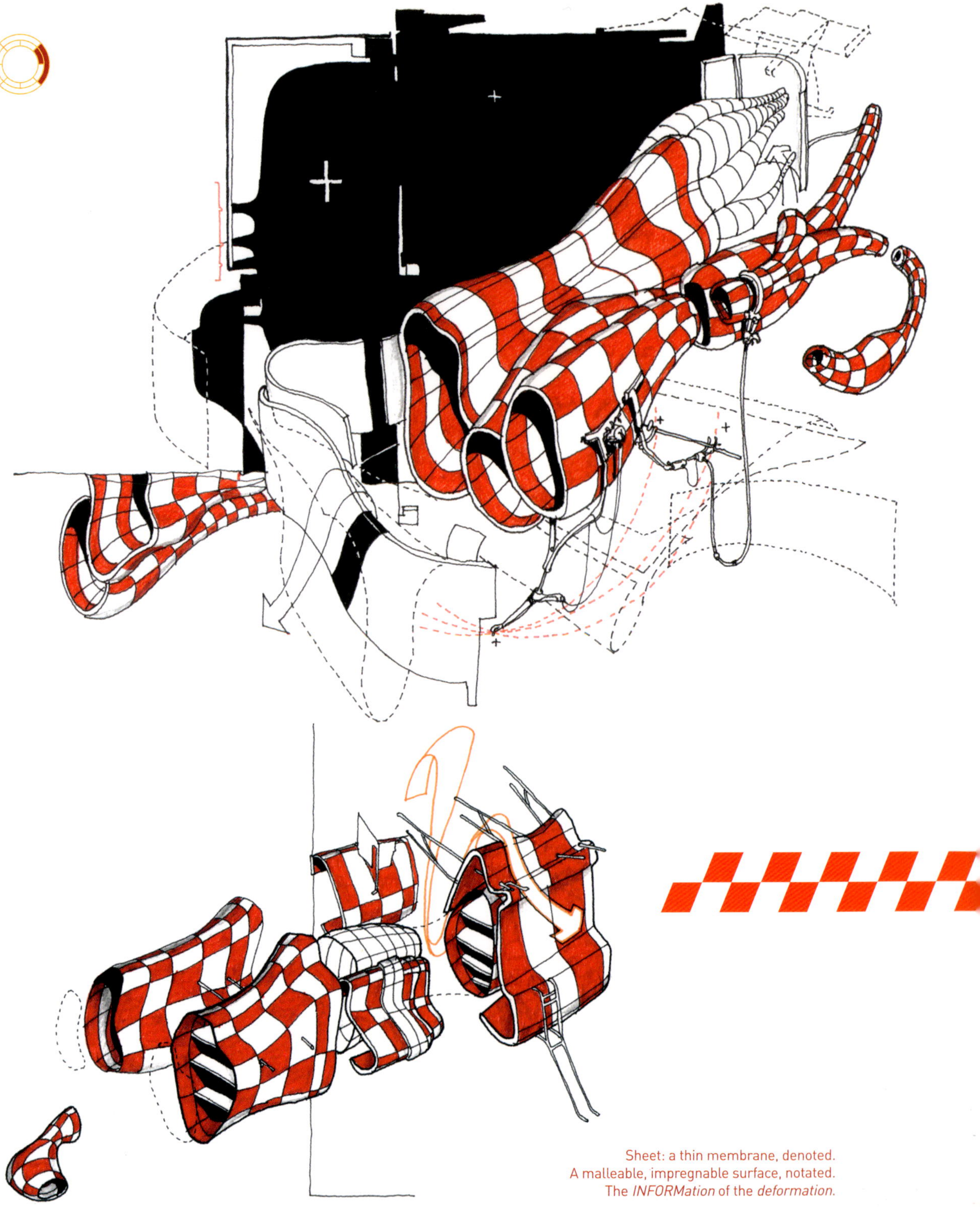

Sheet: a thin membrane, denoted.
A malleable, impregnable surface, notated.
The *INFORMation* of the *deformation*.

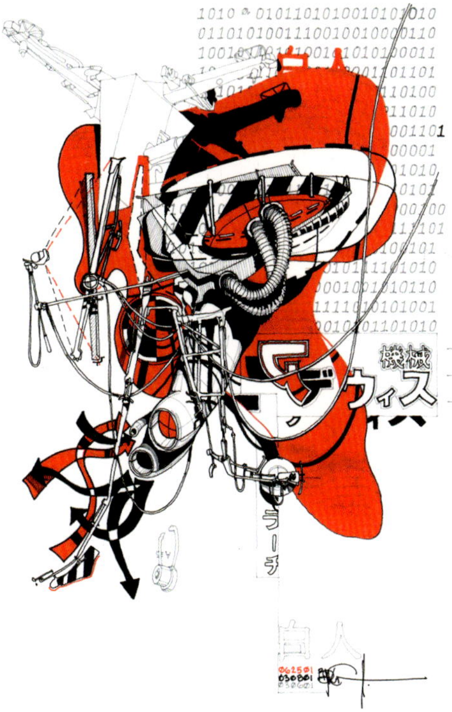
機械
デウィス
ラーチ
白人

A F M

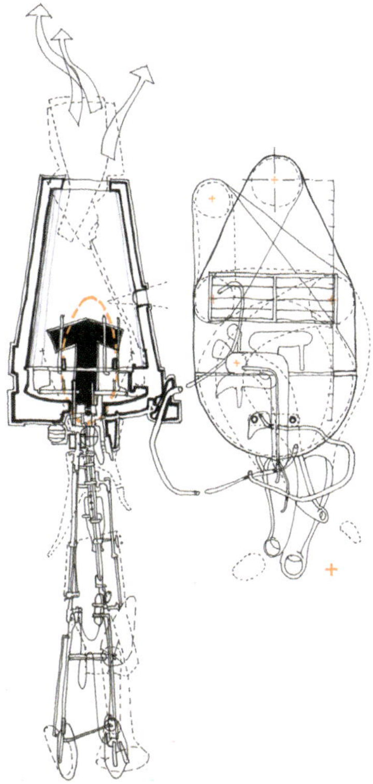

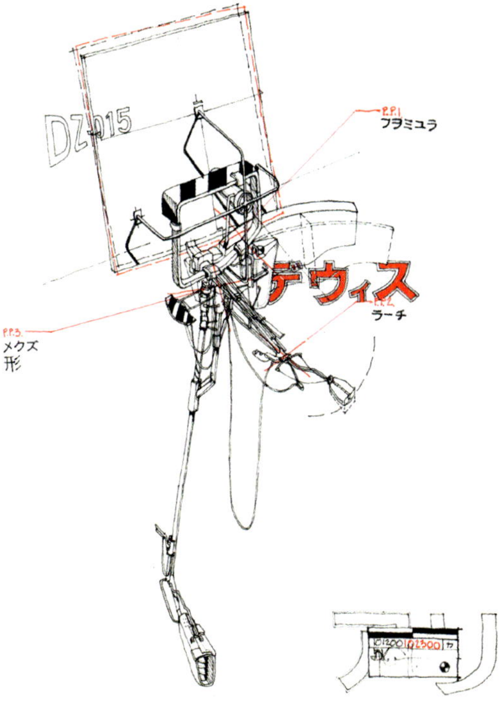
DZ015
P.P.1
フヲミュラ
デウィス
P.P.2
ラーチ
P.P.3.
メクズ
形

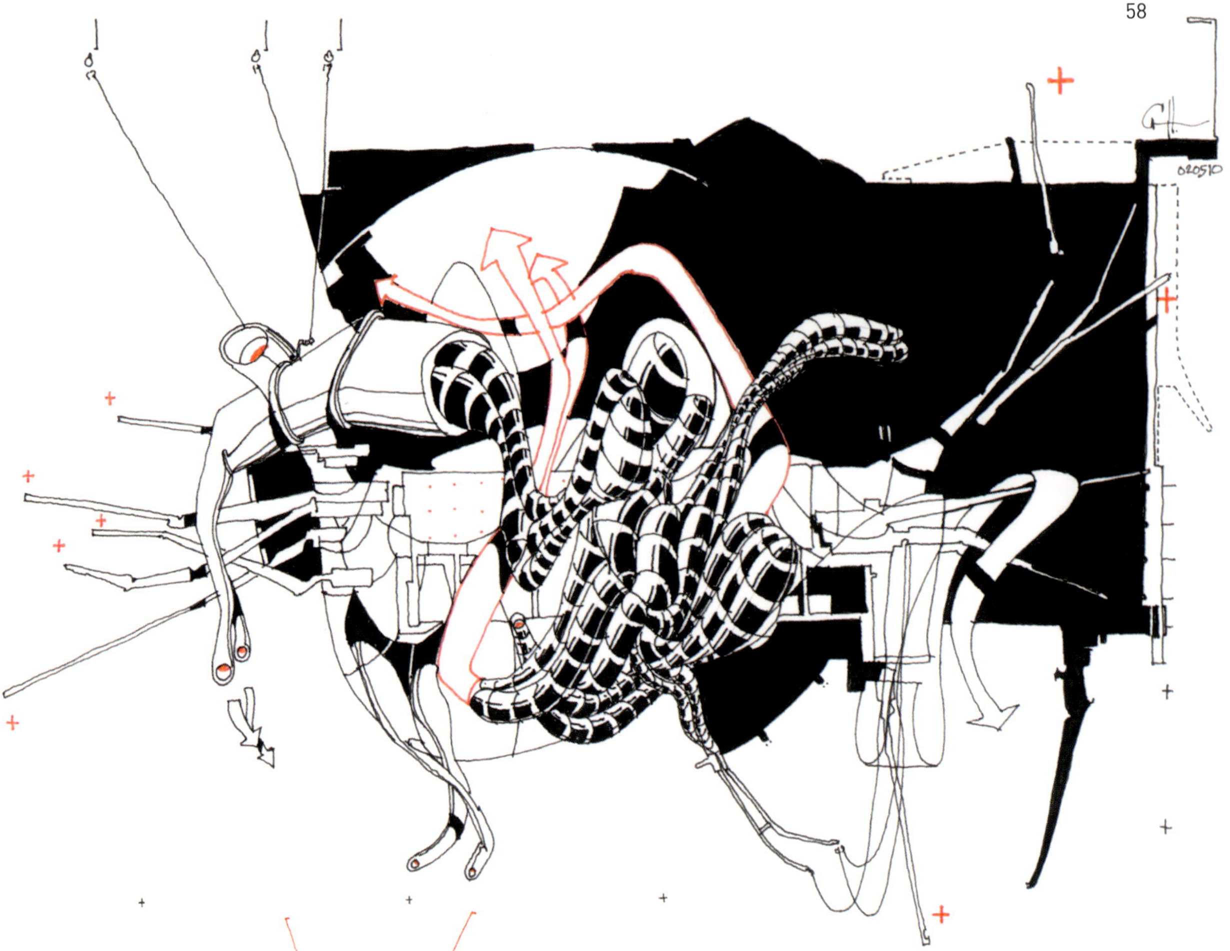

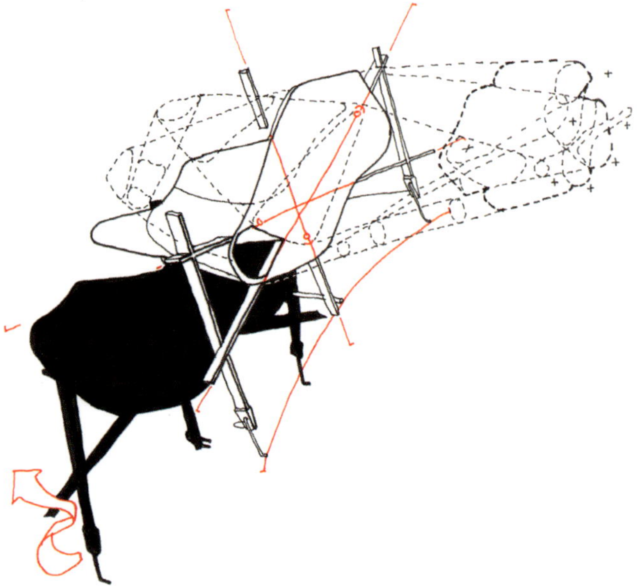

Not so much arti-*fact*, as arti-*fiction*. The structural and spatial properties of the page inform/deForm the entities.

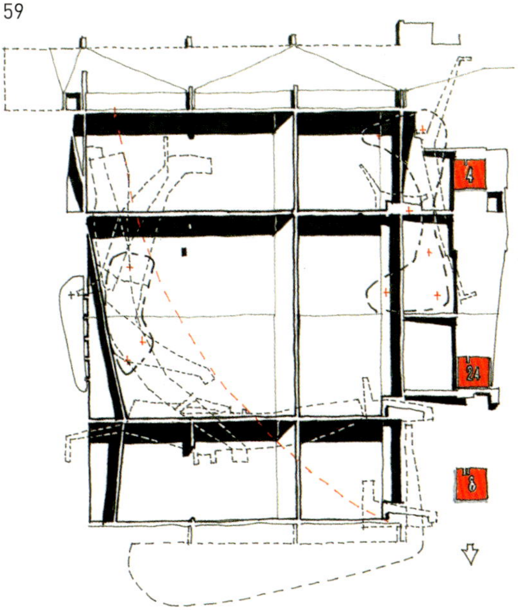

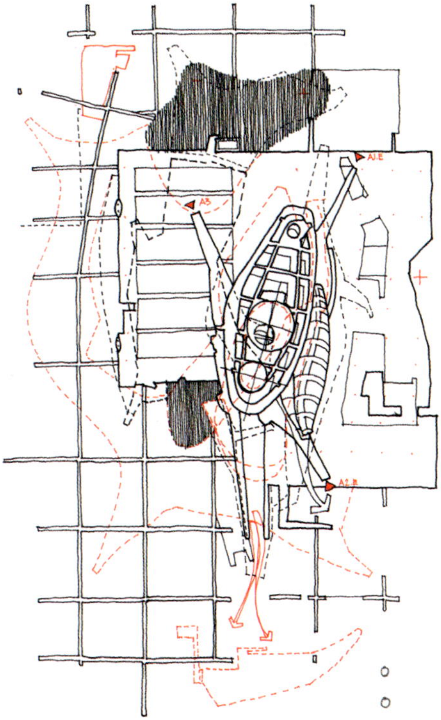

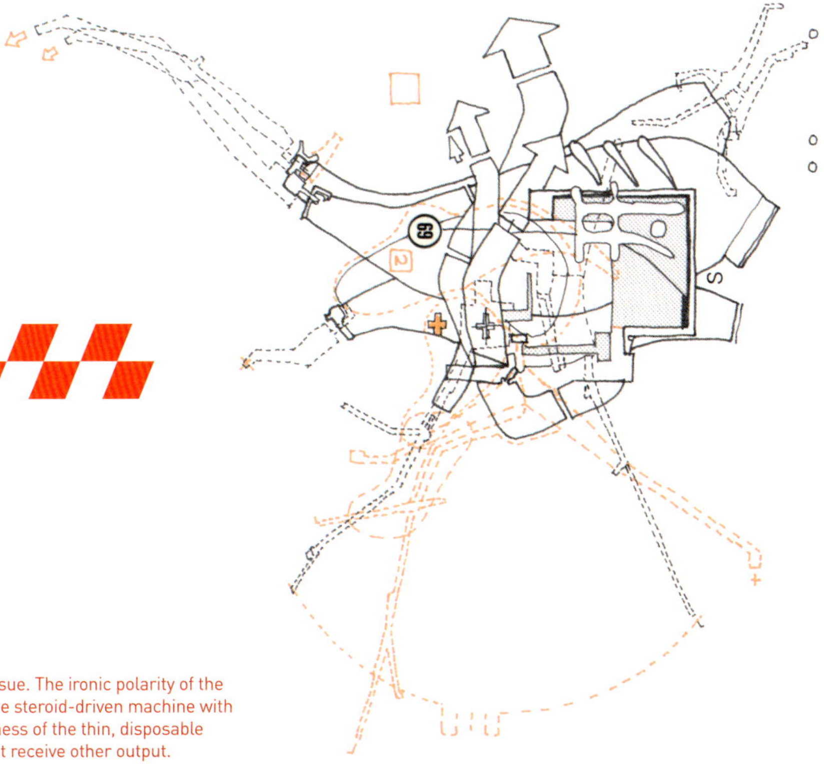

Muscle tissue. The ironic polarity of the mass of the steroid-driven machine with the daintiness of the thin, disposable sheets that receive other output.

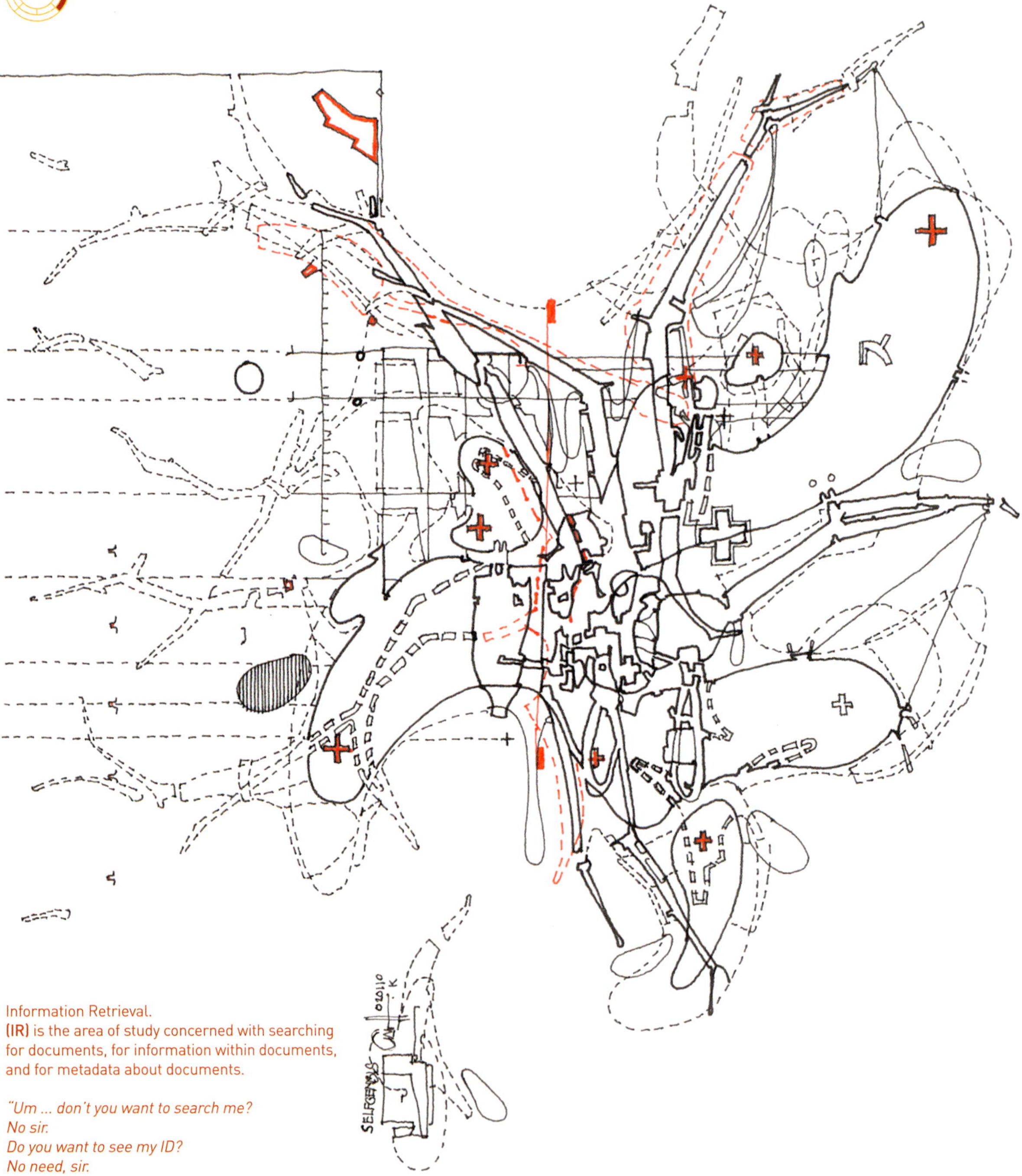

Information Retrieval.
(IR) is the area of study concerned with searching for documents, for information within documents, and for metadata about documents.

"Um … don't you want to search me?
No sir.
Do you want to see my ID?
No need, sir.
But I could be anybody.
No you couldn't sir. This is Information Retrieval."
Brazil (1985)

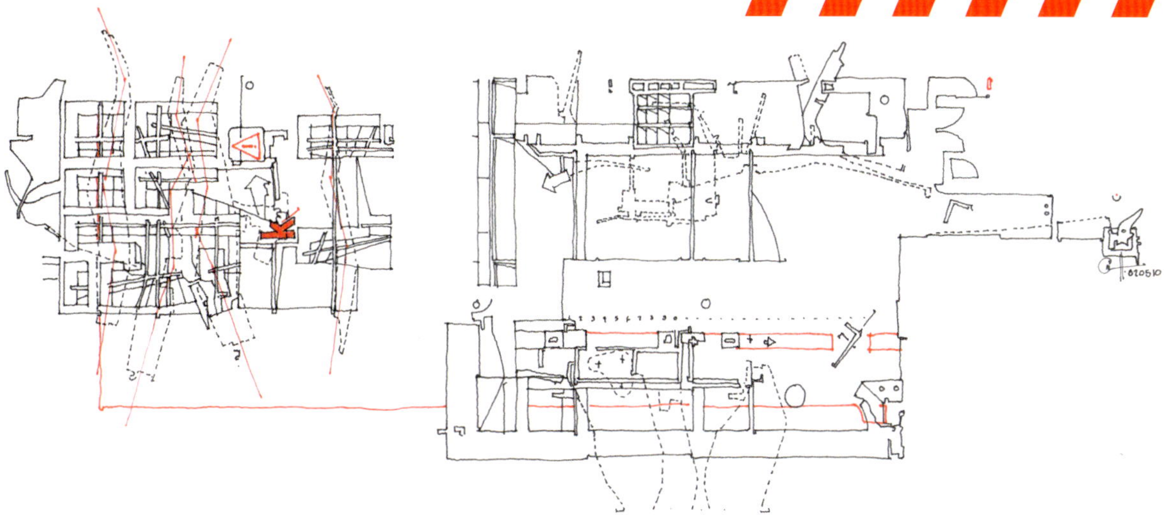
820510

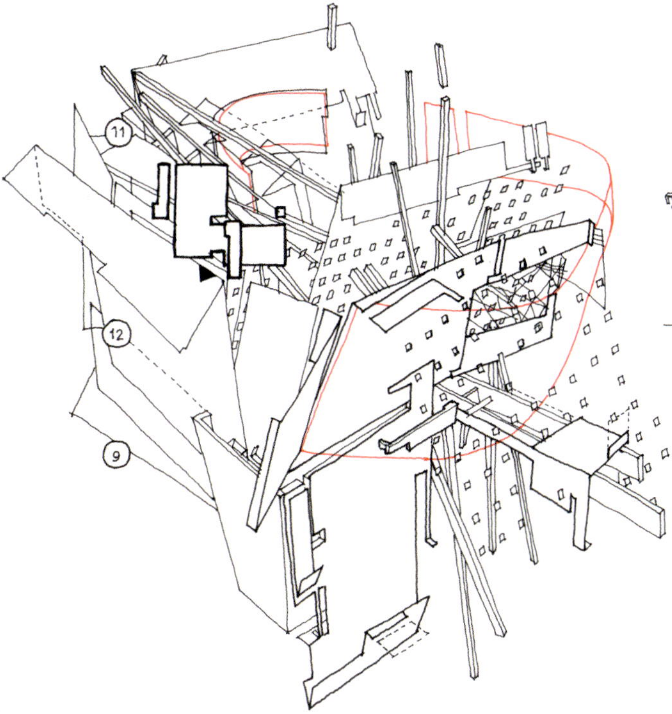
11
12
9

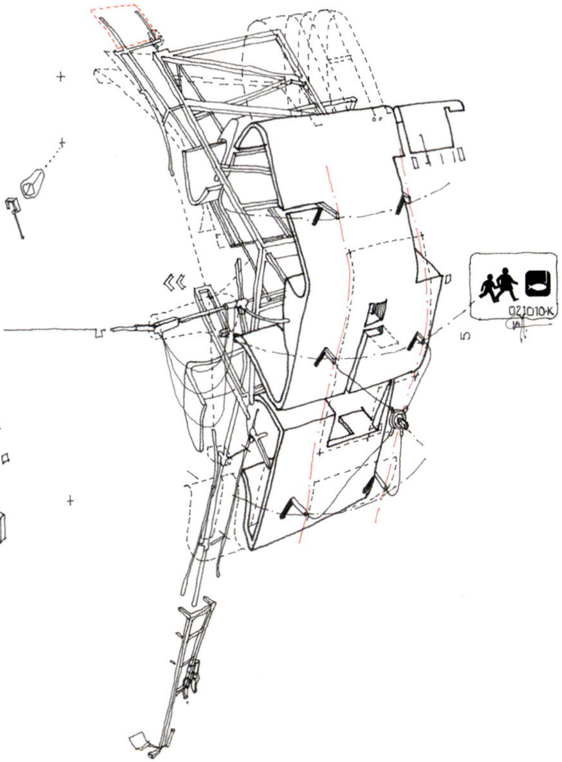
021010-K

Sequence distortion. Similar to projecting the 180 degrees of a triangle on the curved surface of a balloon to get a different sum total of the angles ... or to the Stephen Holtzman reference to the "Cage-ish" experience of the *sherpa* listening to the distortion of "noise" BETWEEN the radio stations' "music" ...

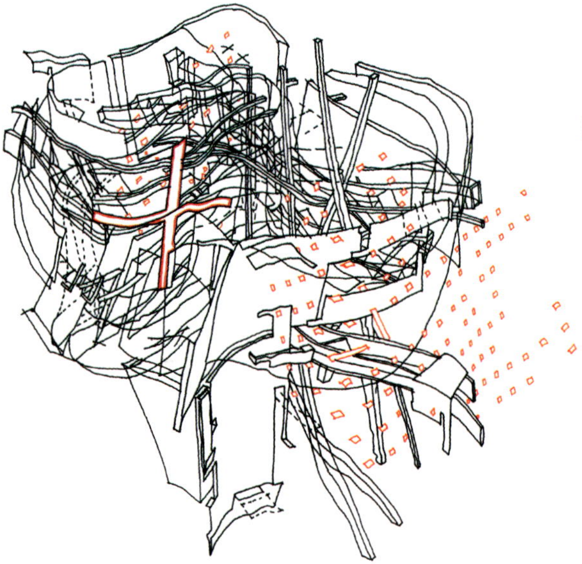

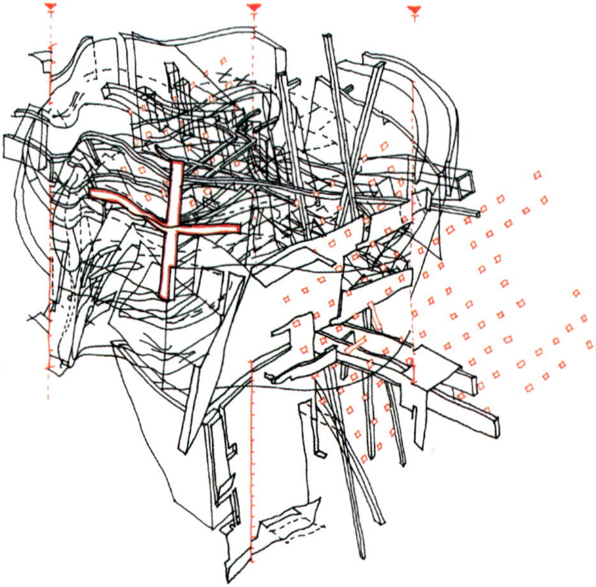

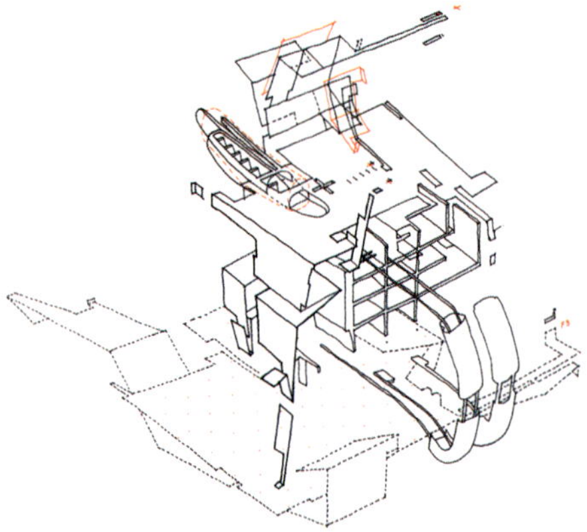

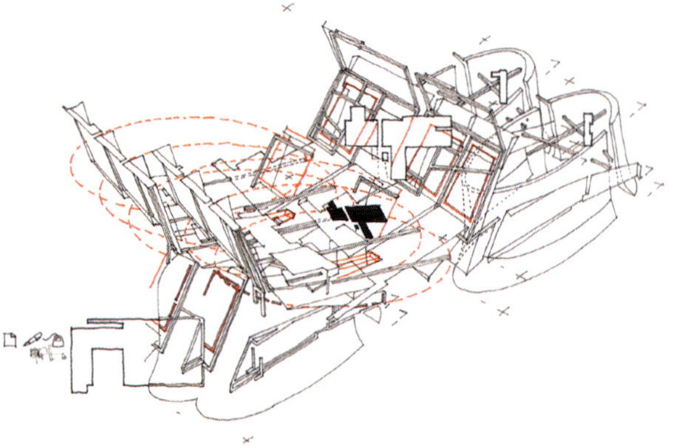

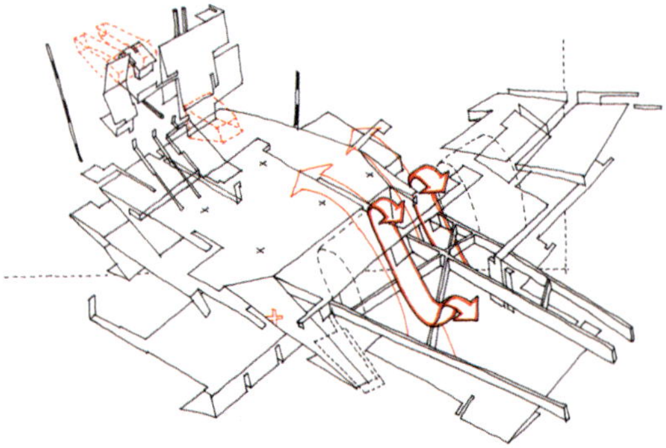

Such is the idea of interfering with the transmission of both the act of drawing with the act of documentation.

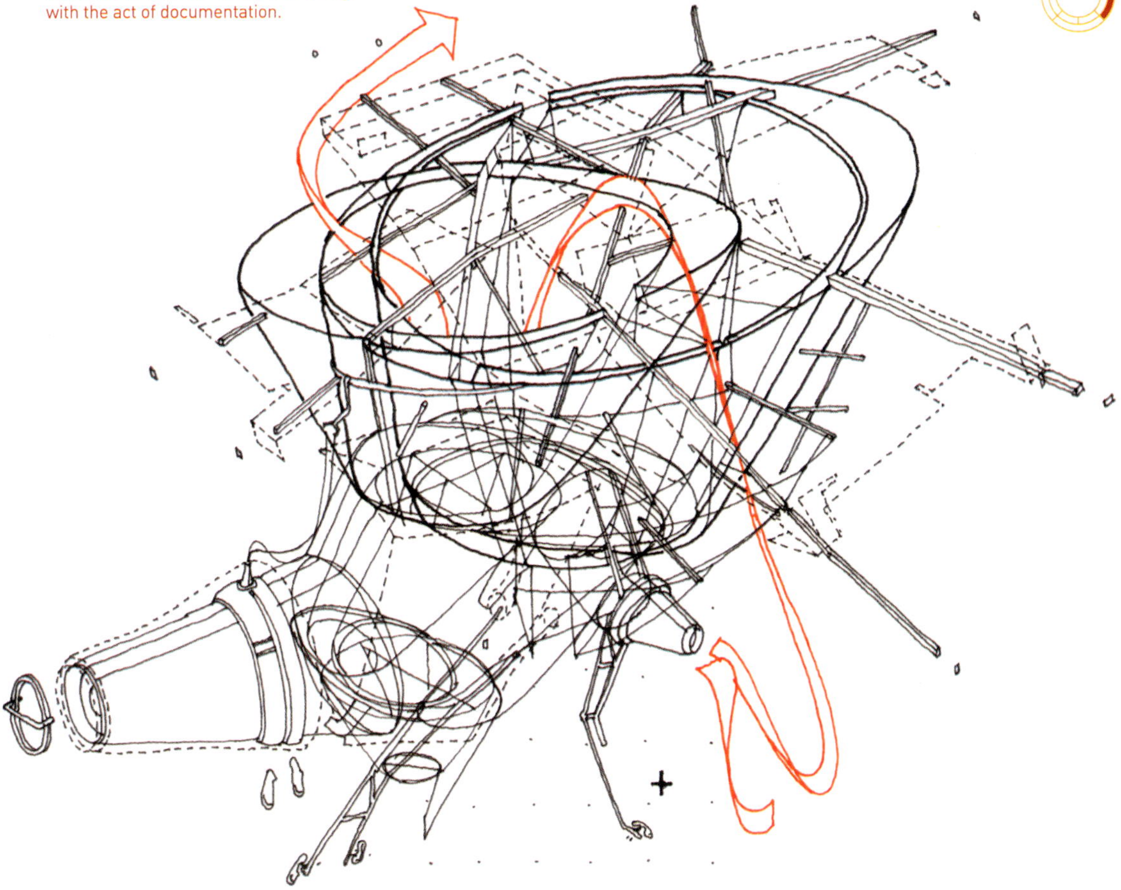

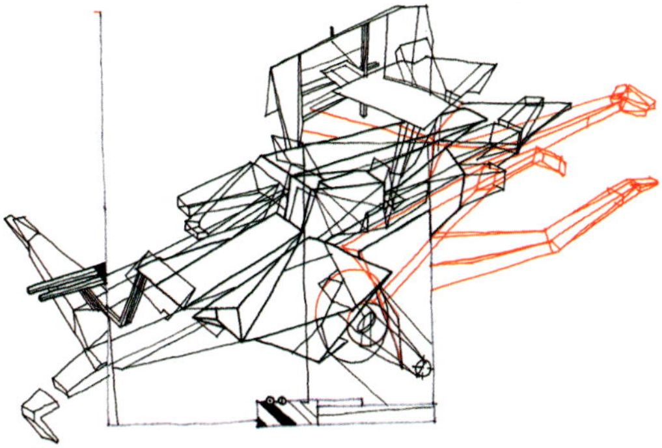

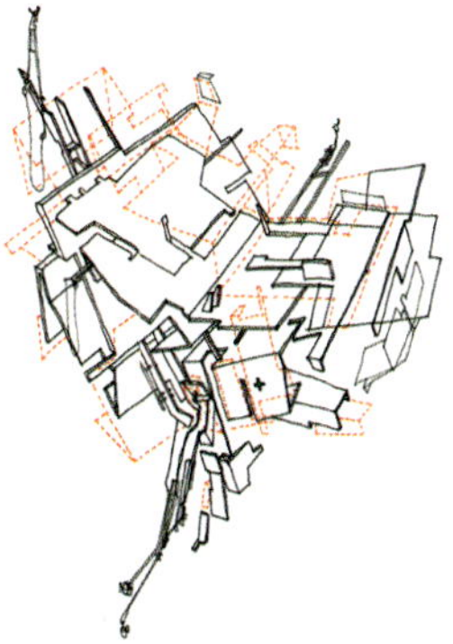

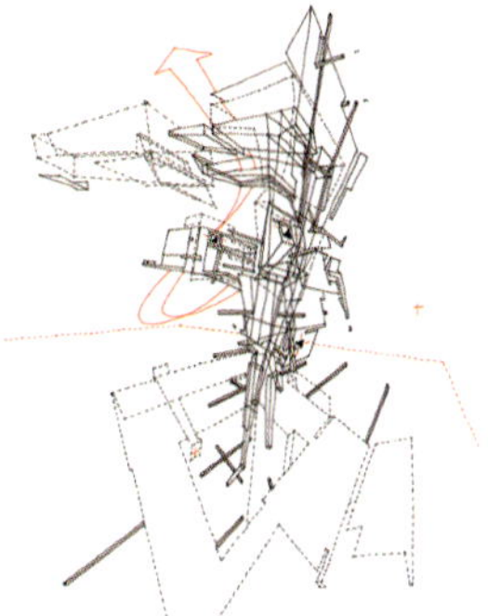

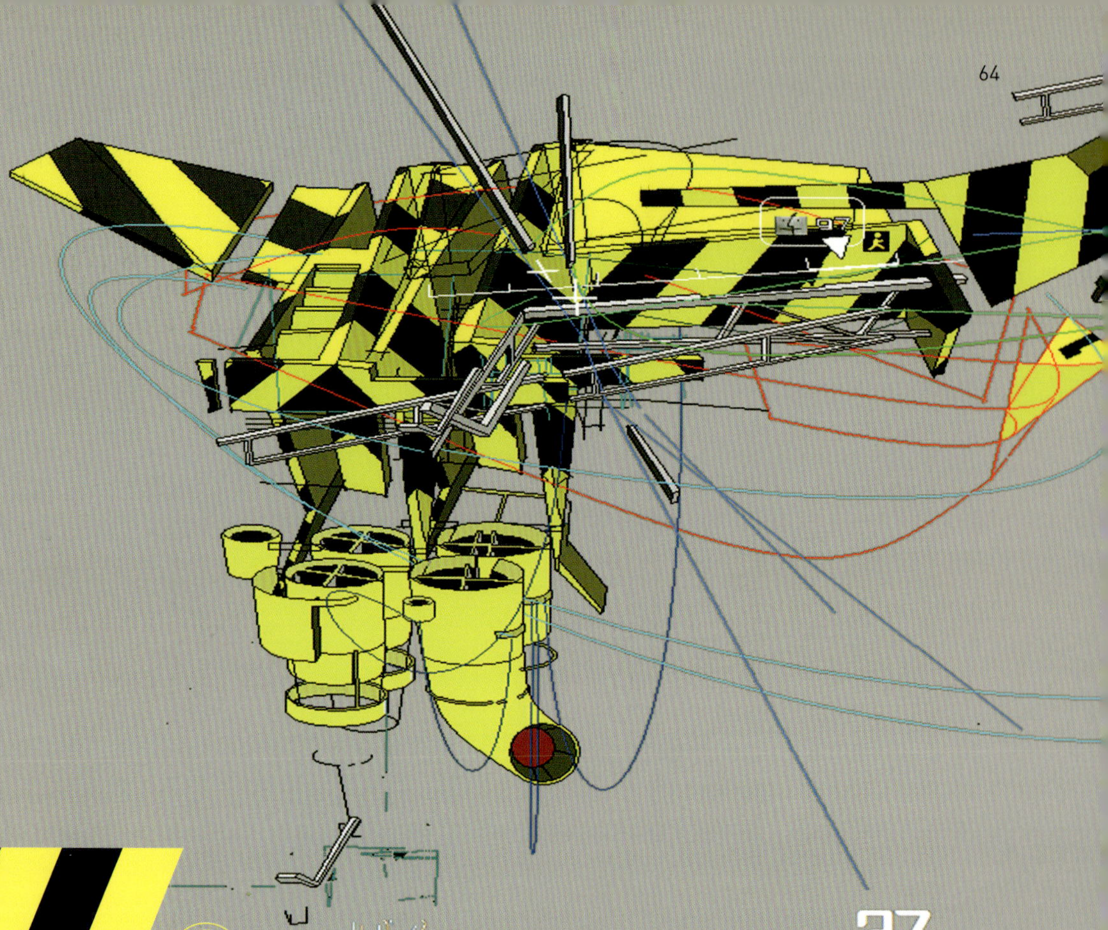

07

Digital Paper®

Pen tablets utilize a stylus, recalling the not-too-distant muscle-memory of pen on paper, and ask us to imagine new tactics not limited by convention or input material. A new typology emerges. Not only was the technique unique [as one develops contextually unique techniques for the playing of acoustic vs. electric guitars], but the outcome was surprisingly dissimilar.

The computer tends to lure us into believing that the digital process is always a state of "being finished." This series attempts to use the PROCESS of digital drawing. The pen tablet is understood as a *DISRUPTIVE TECHNOLOGY* – a foreign system intruding into a natural condition of hand to paper. It is also a producer of *Simultaneity*™ – the space located between dimensions that informs and disrupts them both. It describes an architecture that exists in more than three dimensions, physically + conceptually: the Cartesian System of in-front and behind and the N-Dimensional system of time and duration. The result is an opportunity for select elements from each of the dimensions to interact and disrupt each other, invoking an independent simultaneity, where different views of the same object may be drawn on top of each other, mimicking a "live-active layering."

The Digital Paper series were supported mainly by the *TabletKiosk* Corporation. The body of work was also supported by the Fujitsu PC Corporation. This series was the recipient of a Graham Foundation grant. The images were all constructed "freehand" with WindowsPaint.

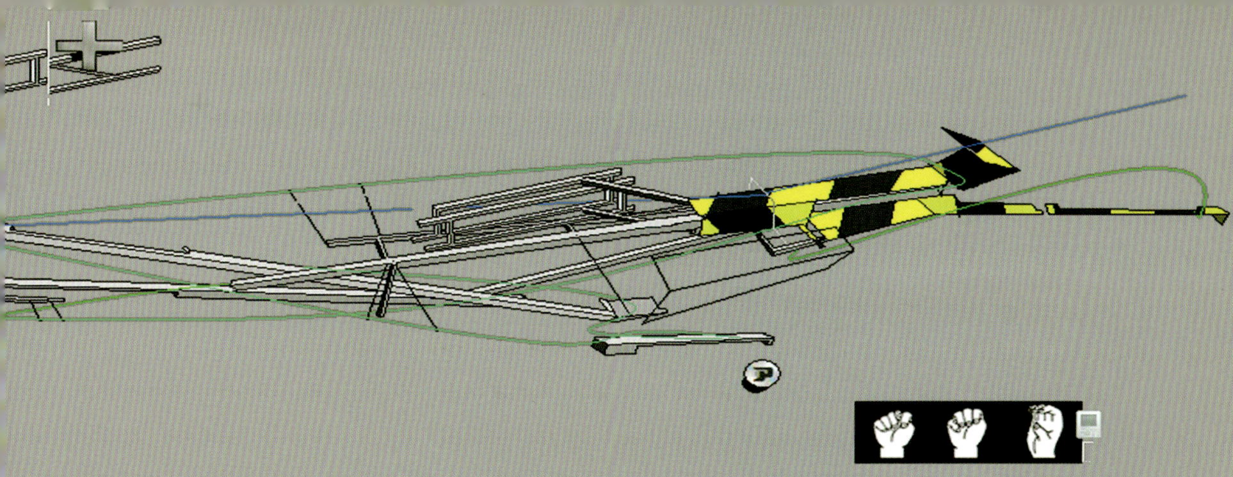

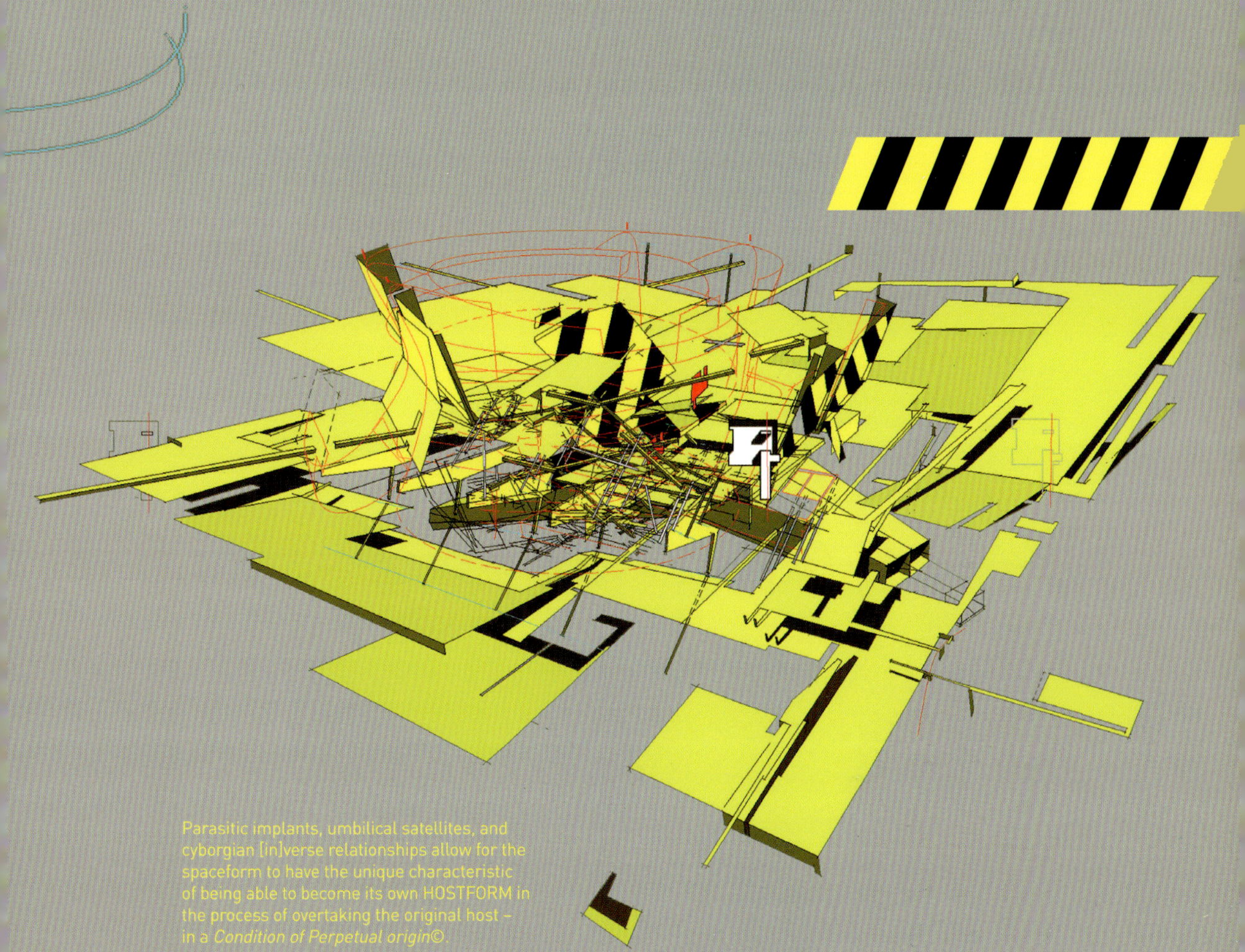

Parasitic implants, umbilical satellites, and cyborgian [in]verse relationships allow for the spaceform to have the unique characteristic of being able to become its own HOSTFORM in the process of overtaking the original host – in a *Condition of Perpetual origin©*.

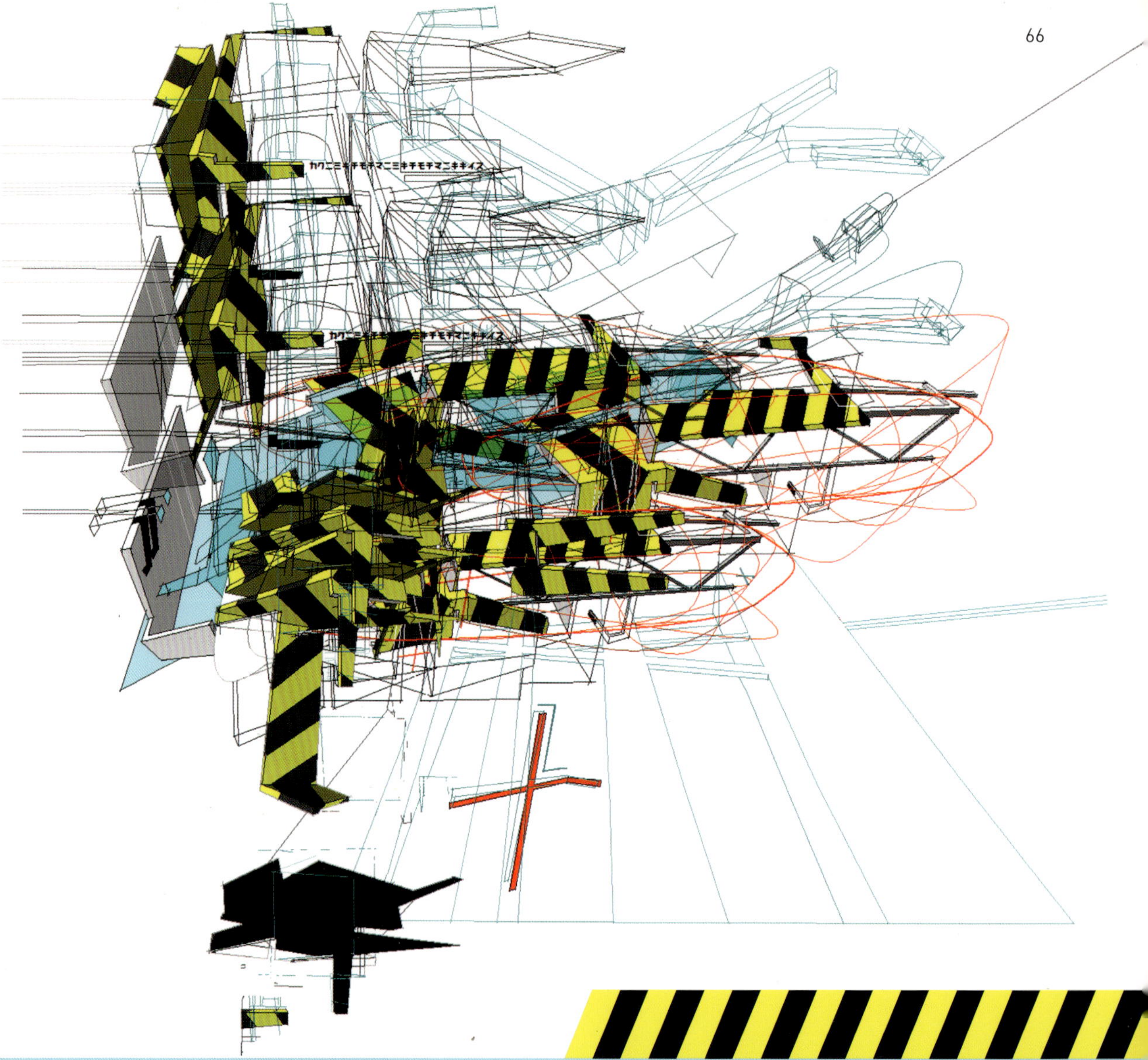
カワニミキチモチマニミキチモチマニキキイス

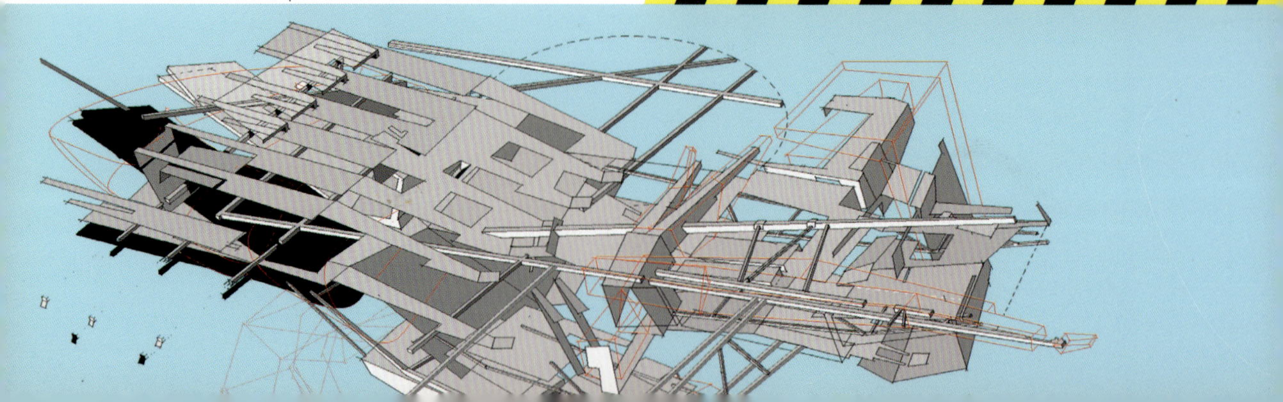

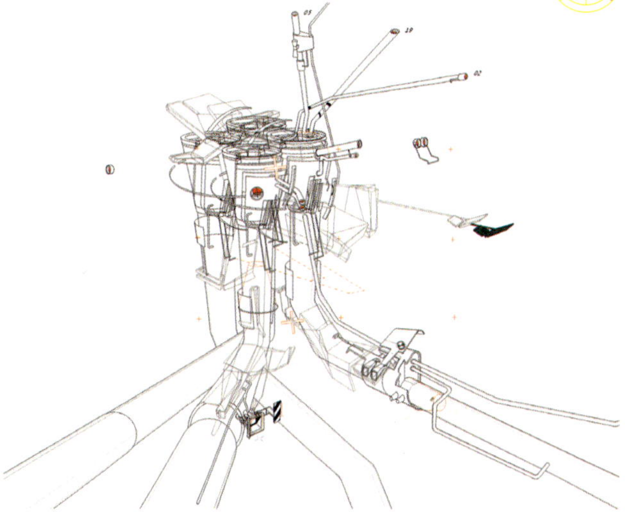

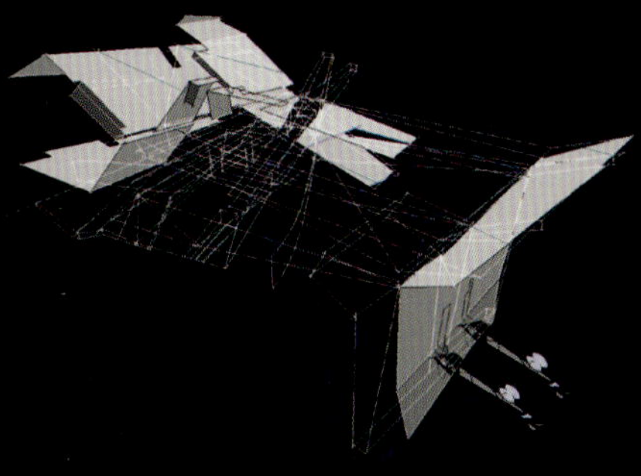

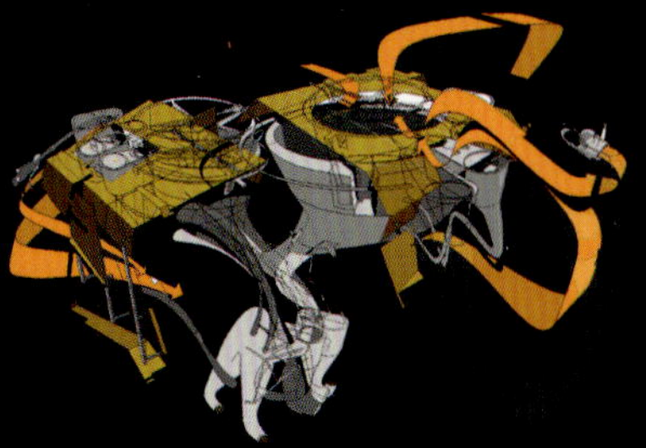

Digital Stratigraphy, via pixel drawing. No paper was harmed in the execution of these images. No 3D modeling was used in the generation of this new archetype. 8-bits never tasted so good.

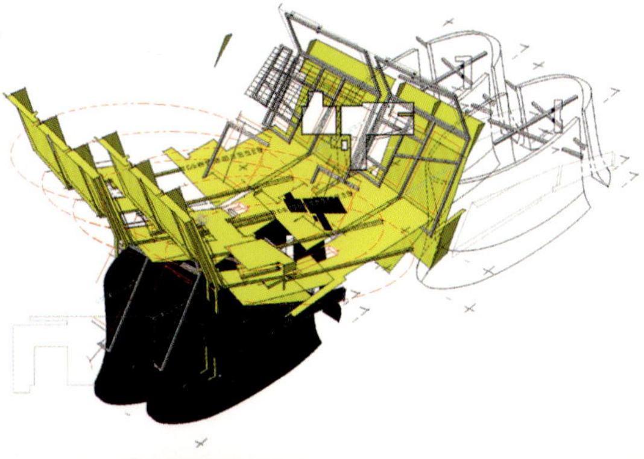

アス機械
digital paper ©
形

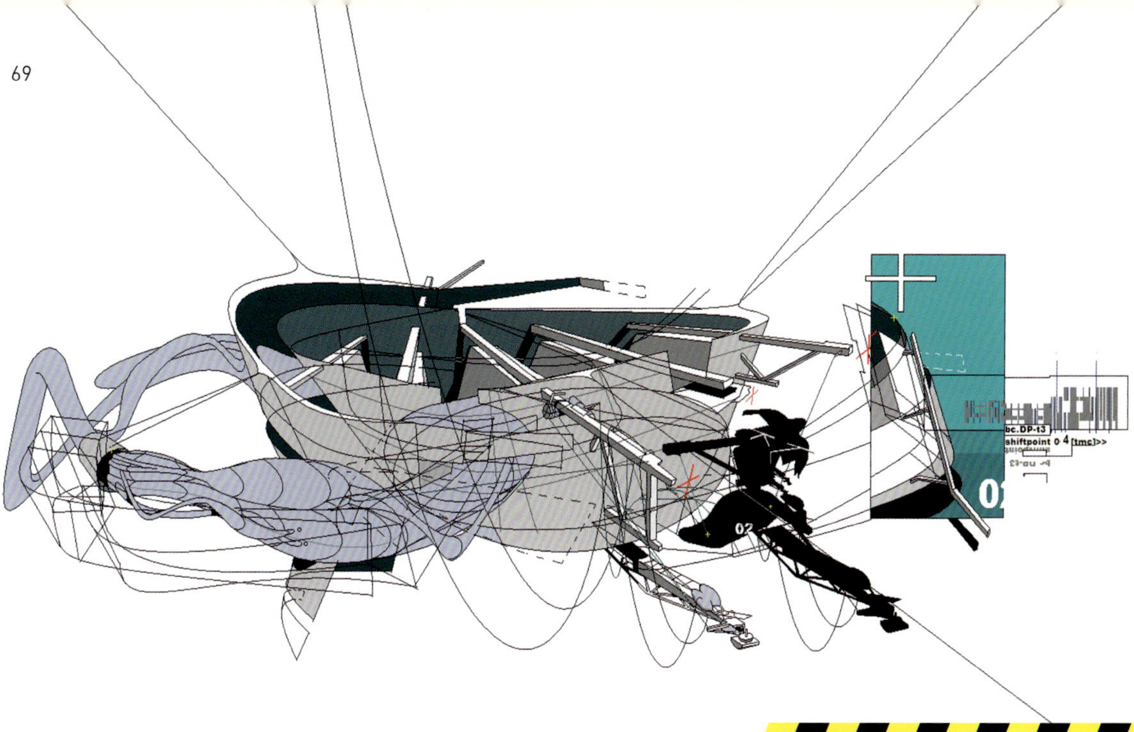

Though the receptacle media has no measurable Cartesian depth, the screen is still a 2-dimensional laboratory for line impregnation. Steroid sketchbooks. Pneudraulic pixels. **i-mages.**

Dimensional Shifting™ vibrates between the reality of spatial occupation and the nature of construction. Cartesian overlap explores the view of simultaneous realms of perception.

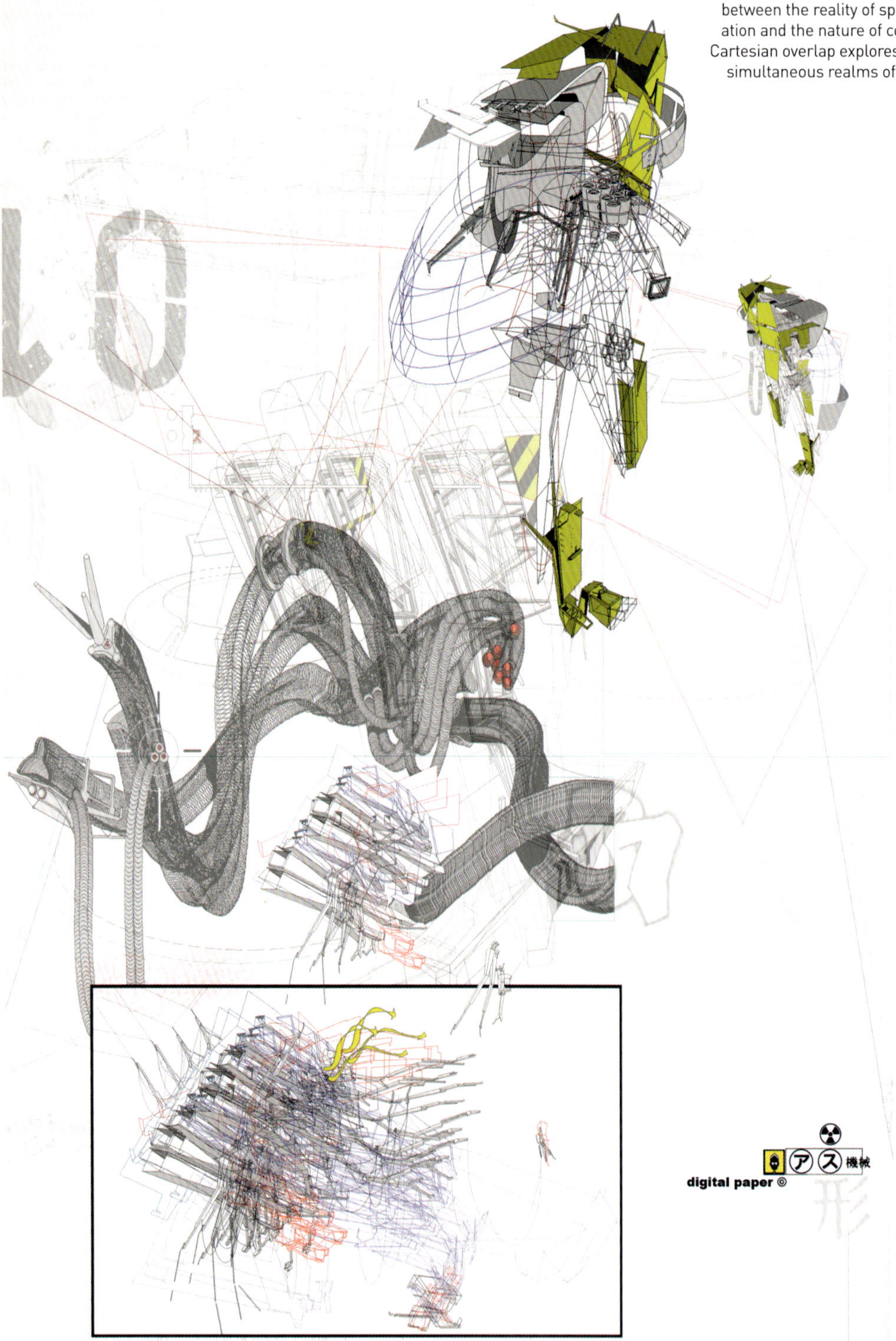

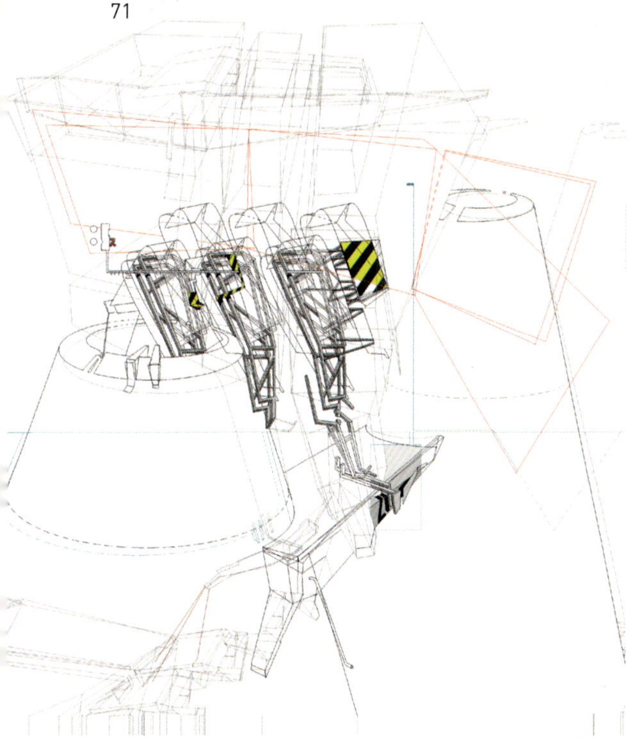

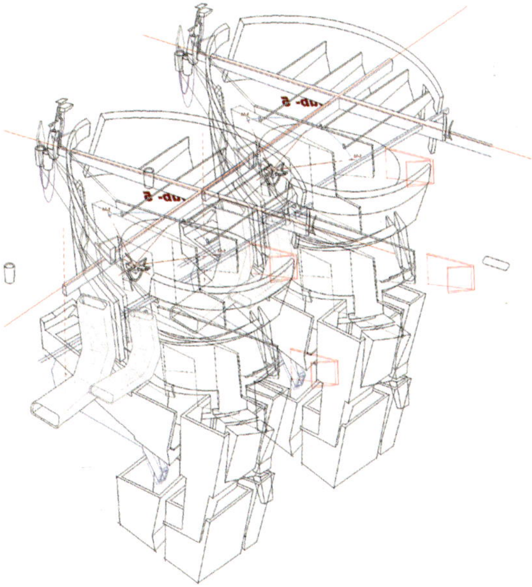

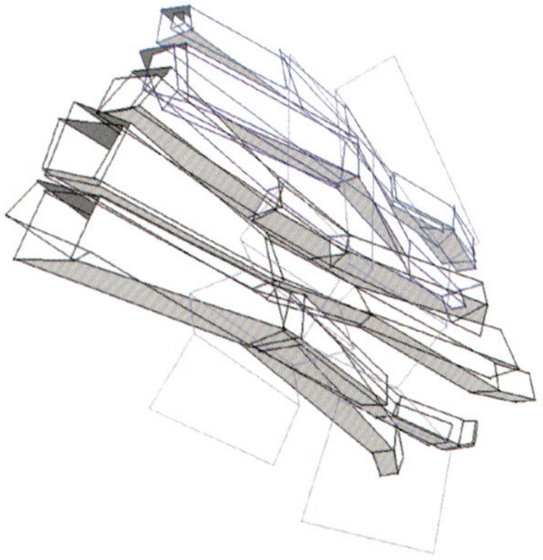

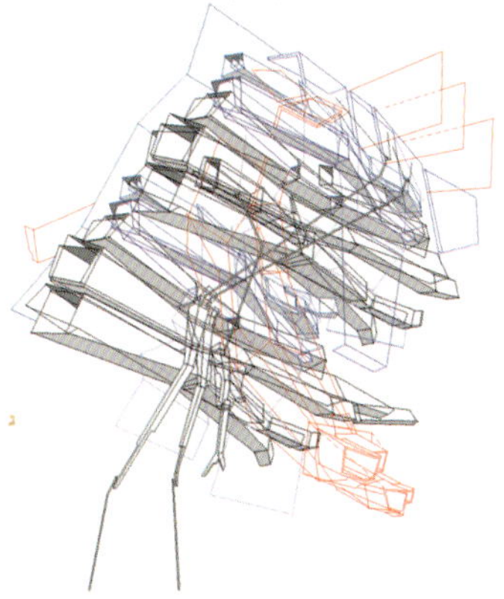

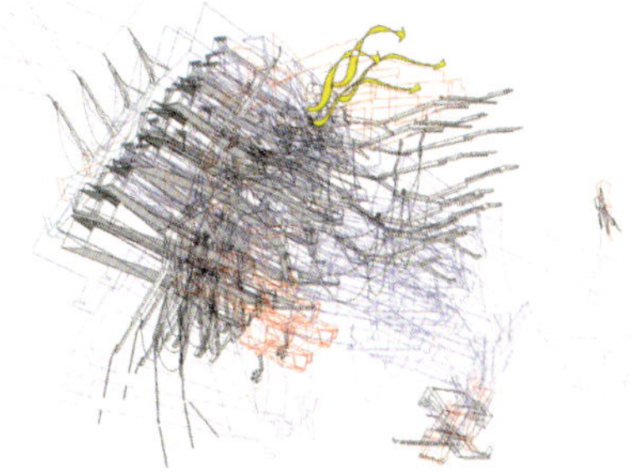

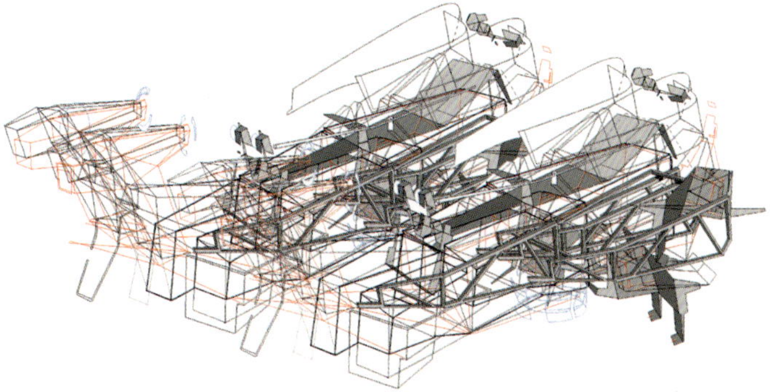

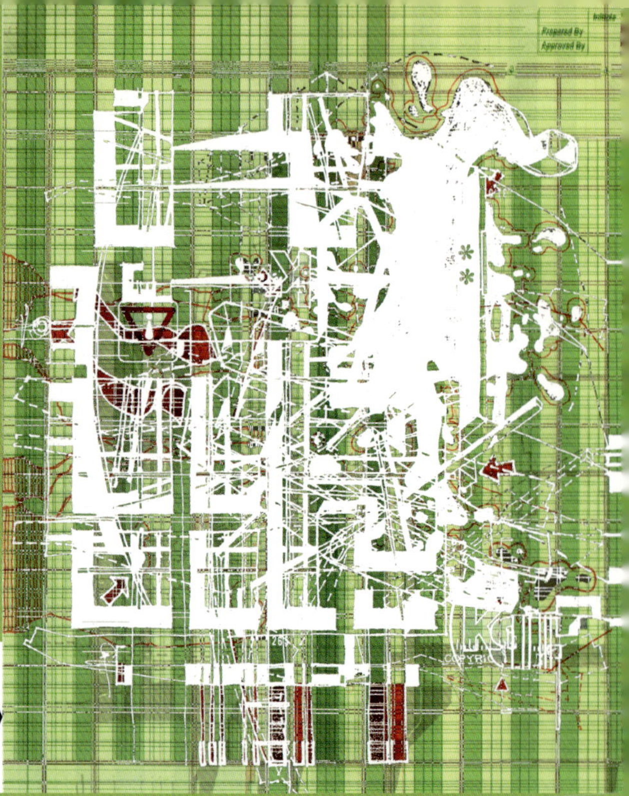

Greensheets/ Topo:Typo

For this investigation, **native paper** refers to the preprinted forms used for various data-input situations – spreadsheets, inventory lists, accounting ledgers, etc. Architecturally, the extension from **page** to **site** is a natural one. The notion of finding or seeing information about any given condition is seen as the premise to a more complete experiment.

What are implications of the infection of a ***non-native typology*** into an existing ***surface typography***?

A ledger book does not typically receive information other than text, and rarely does it receive information **in** or **at** places other than the designated cells. That goes against its purpose. Once one incorrectly enters information – one ignores the inference of the native page function.

If we express the definition of "page" as: *to summon or alert by electronic pager, or to control an electrical appliance or machine, remotely by means of an electronic signal*, then we can begin to import a more symbolic content of the ideas of Mechudzu, and even the concept that the mark on a surface is indeed the artificial calling of a space/time event, perhaps to the analogy of an archaeological dig of an event that has yet to occur.

Then the use of the term page extends beyond that of paper, and allows for a type of physical and systematic structural exploration that yields a much broader understanding of content as medium vs. the old paradigm that content carries media.

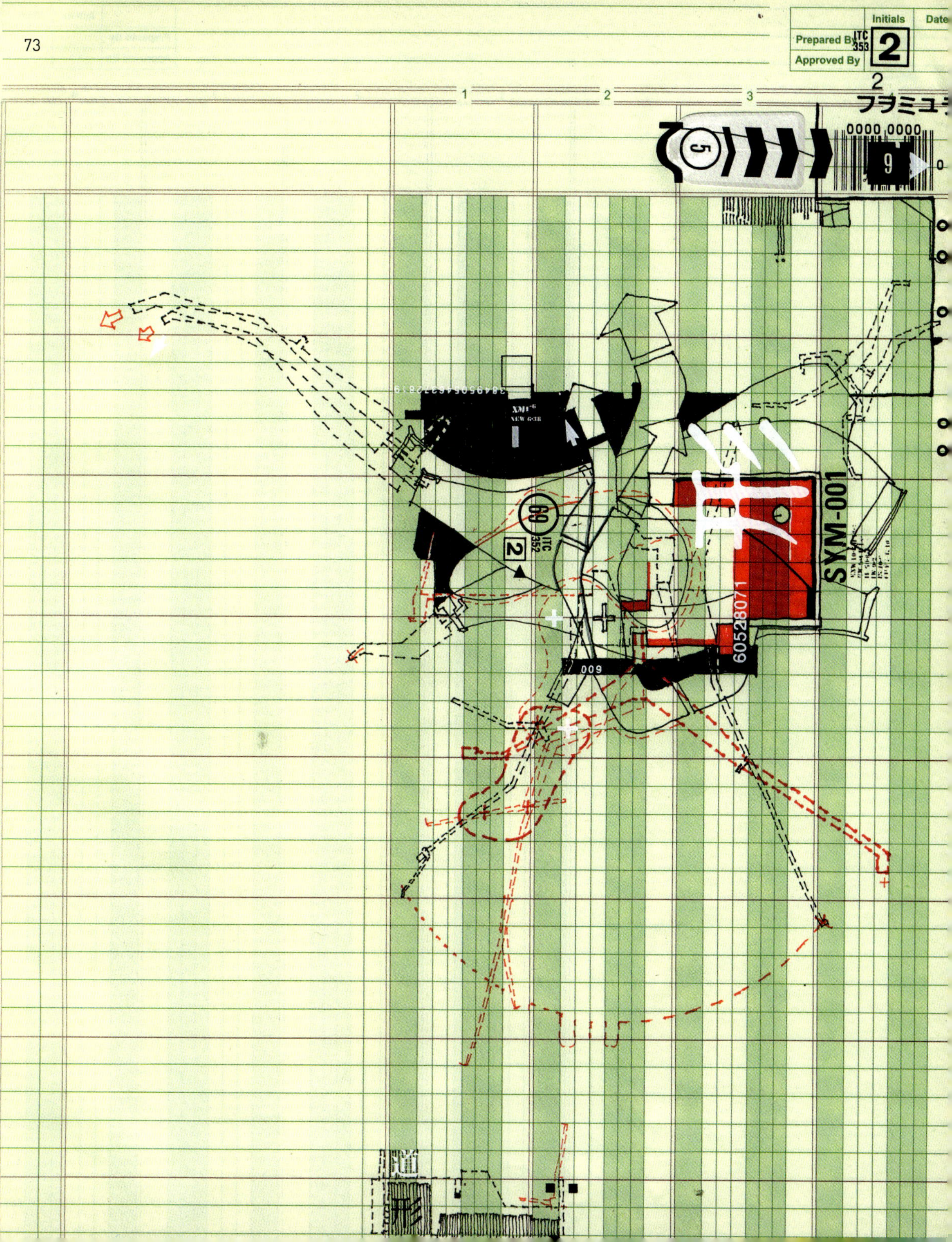
Initials
Date
Prepared By
ITC 353
2
Approved By
2
フヲミュ
0000 0000
9
60
ITC 352
2
SYM-001
60528071
009

Approved By

1 2 3 4

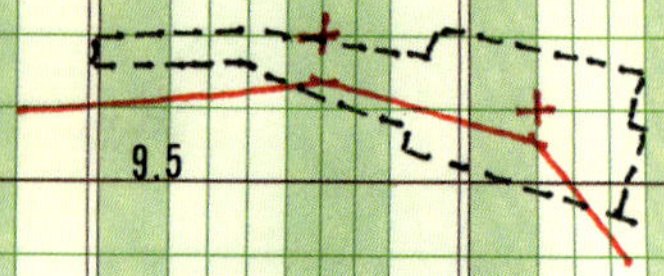

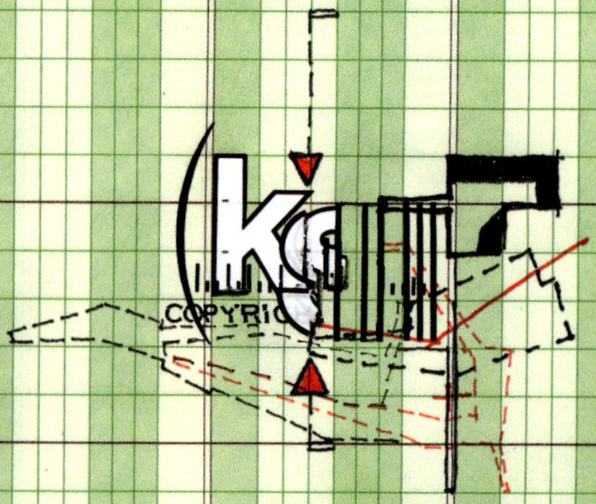

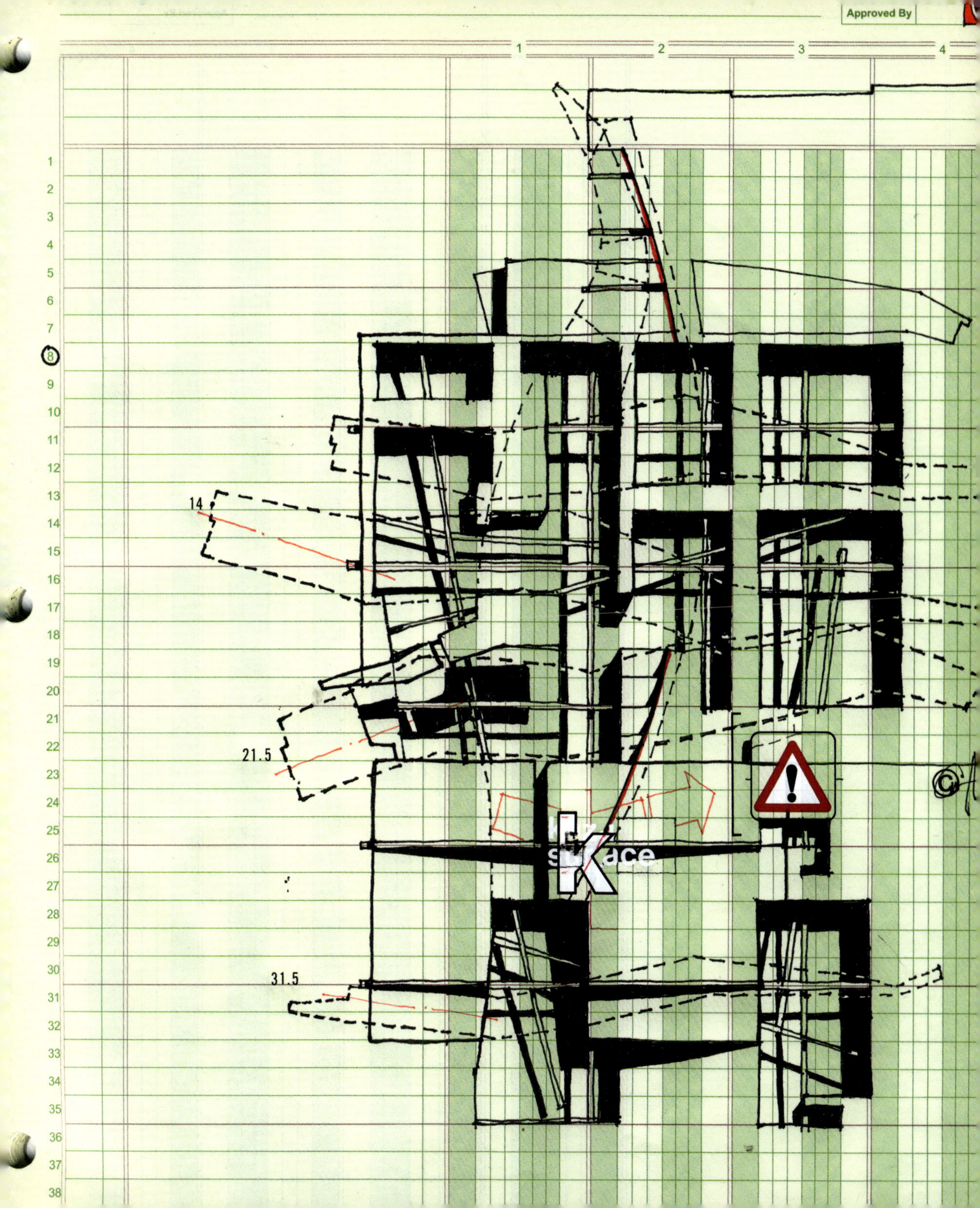
Approved By
14
21.5
31.5

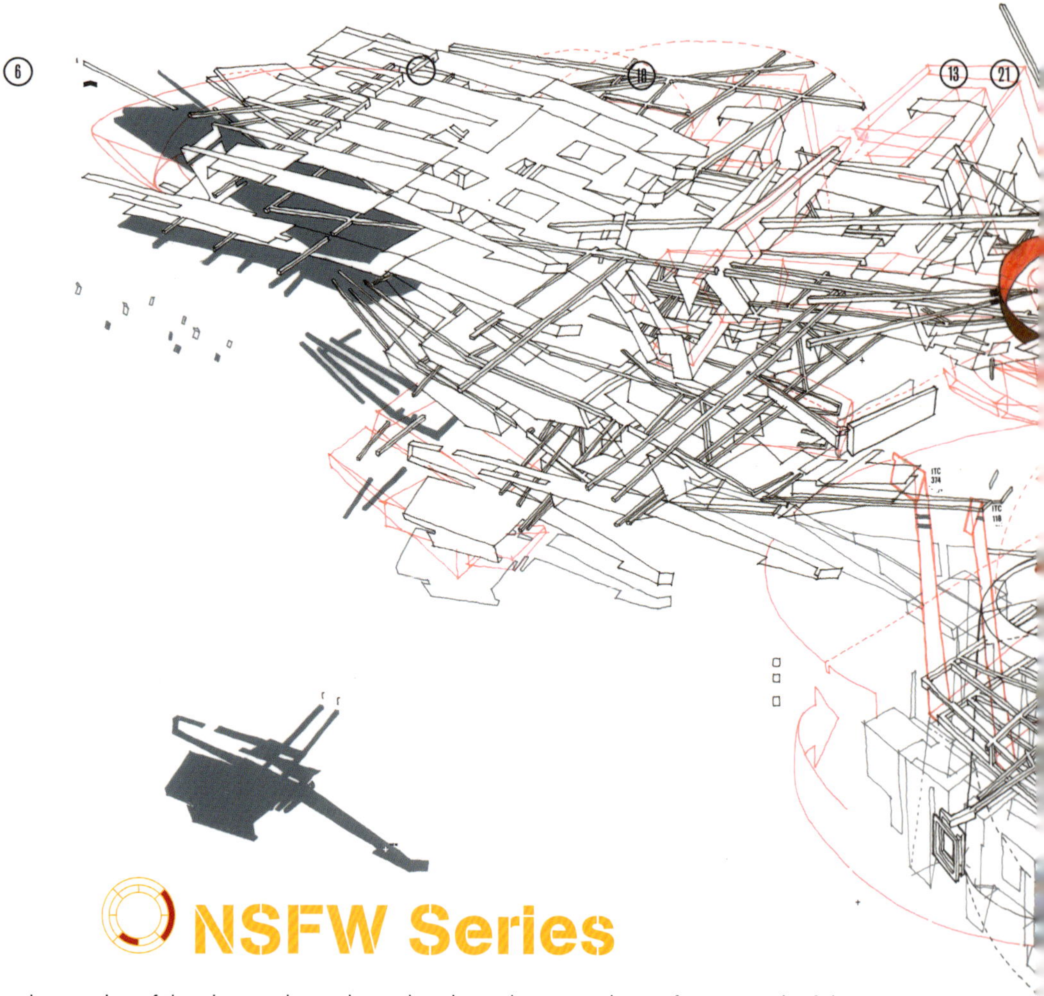

NSFW Series

In search of the elusive destruction of the picture plane, these drawings showcase the surface scratch of the hybrid between that which is *topo*, that which is *typo*, and that which denotes architecture. *Not suitable/safe for work (**NSFW**), not work-suitable/safe (NWS), or not school-suitable (NSS) is Internet slang typically used in e-mail, videos, and on interactive discussion areas (such as AIA events, awards ceremonies, or cocktail parties) to mark URLs or hyperlinks which may be architecturally explicit or include imagery containing experiments, helping the occupant or observer to avoid potentially objectionable content.* Perhaps there are new categories: NSFA [not safe for architecture]; NSFAIA; NSFB [banality]; or just plain ***NS***.

NSFW has particular relevance for individuals conducting research on the Internet at workplaces or communities that have policies prohibiting (even inadvertent) access to architecturally explicit content. Companies and individuals frequently adopt such policies because they regard the presence of architecturally explicit content as a misuse of company property (or education resources) and, potentially, a violation of status quo policy.

These are dangerous. Do not observe without adult supervision. *At no time attempt to inhabit the constructs.*

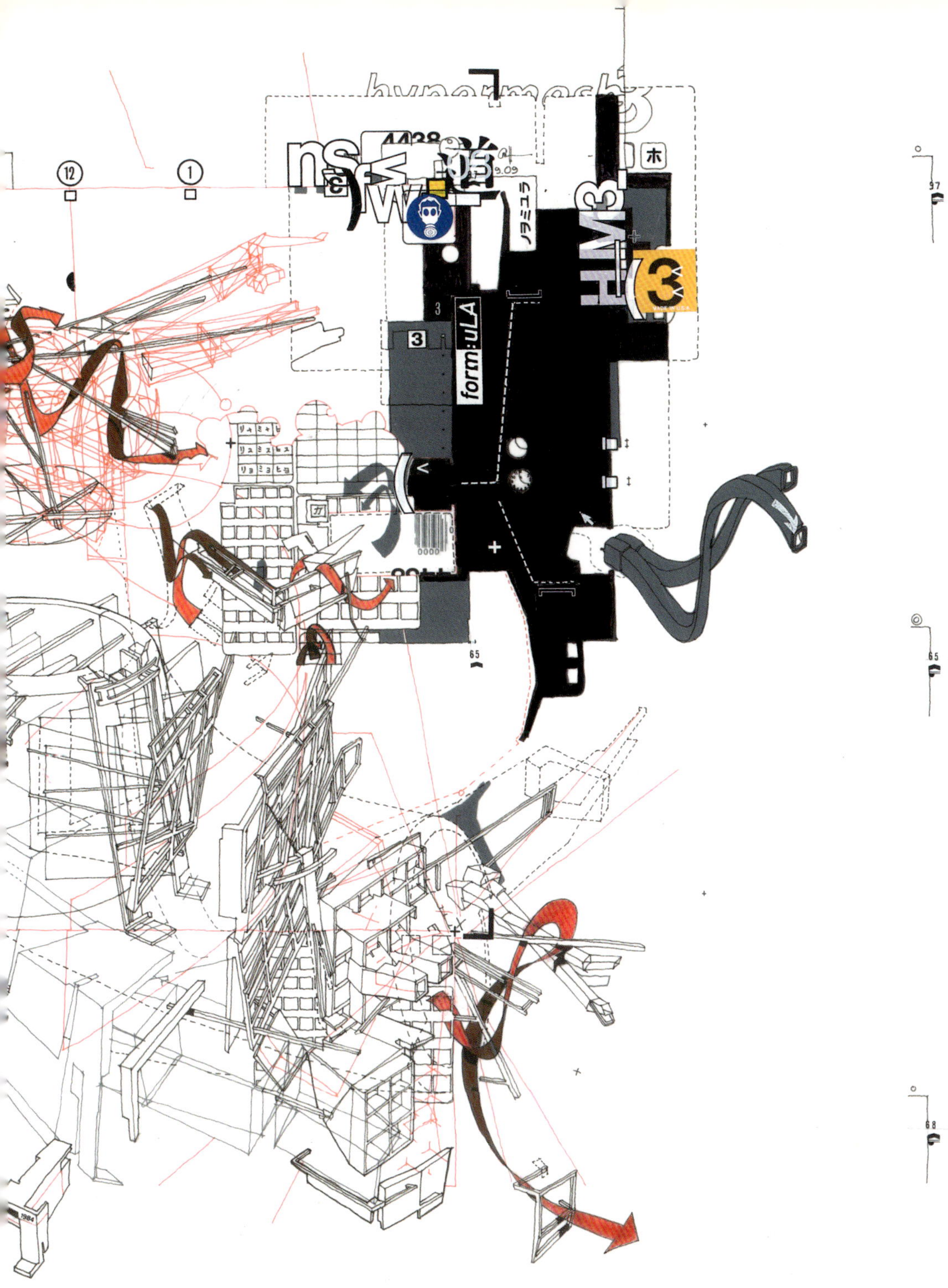
form:uLA
HM3
ノラミユラ
65

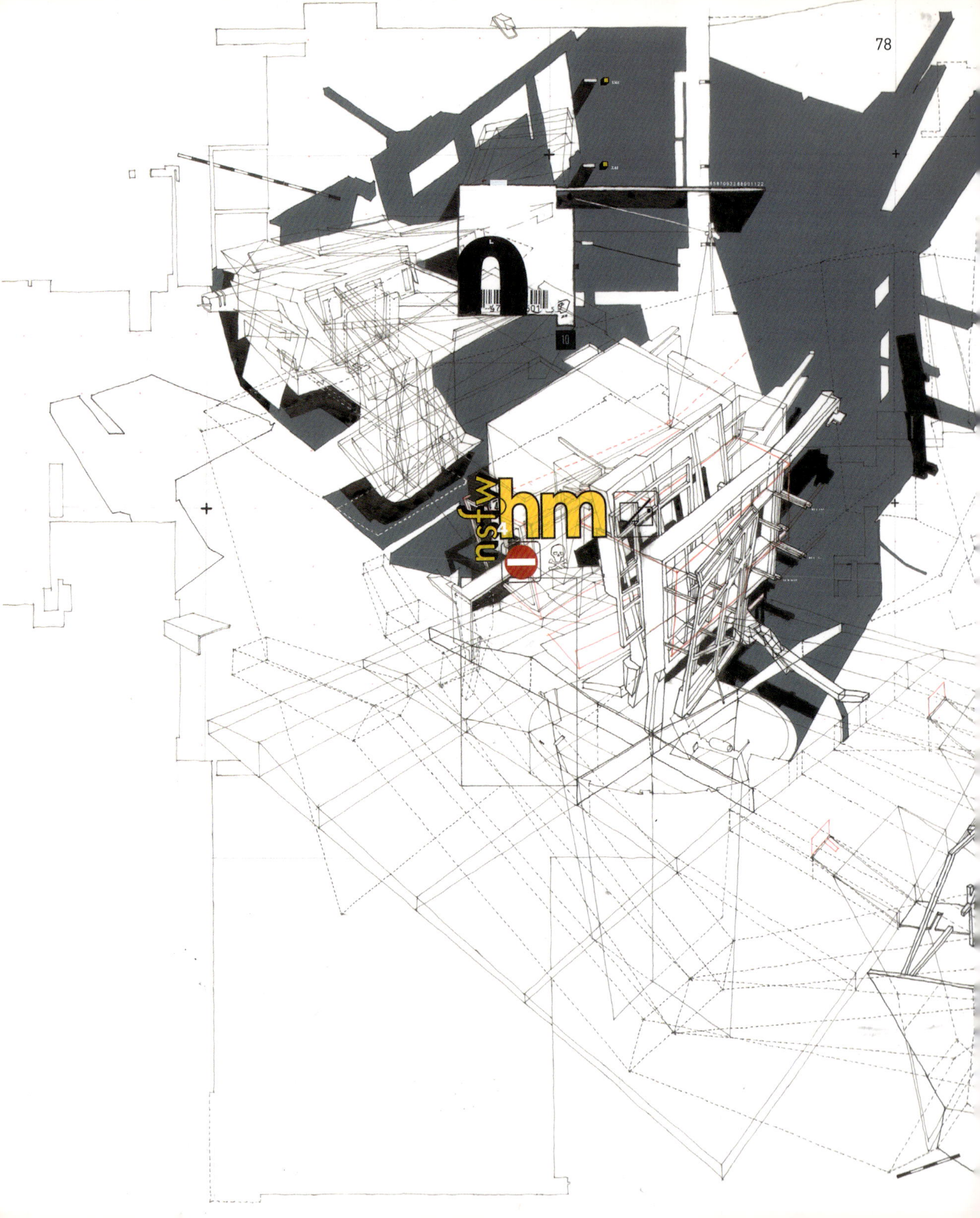
10
hm
nsfw
4

Artificial *surfacescapes* begat the interstitial space of shadow receptors ... as *realspace*. The zone of occupation increases as we begin to understand the architectural configurations of the drawing "surface."

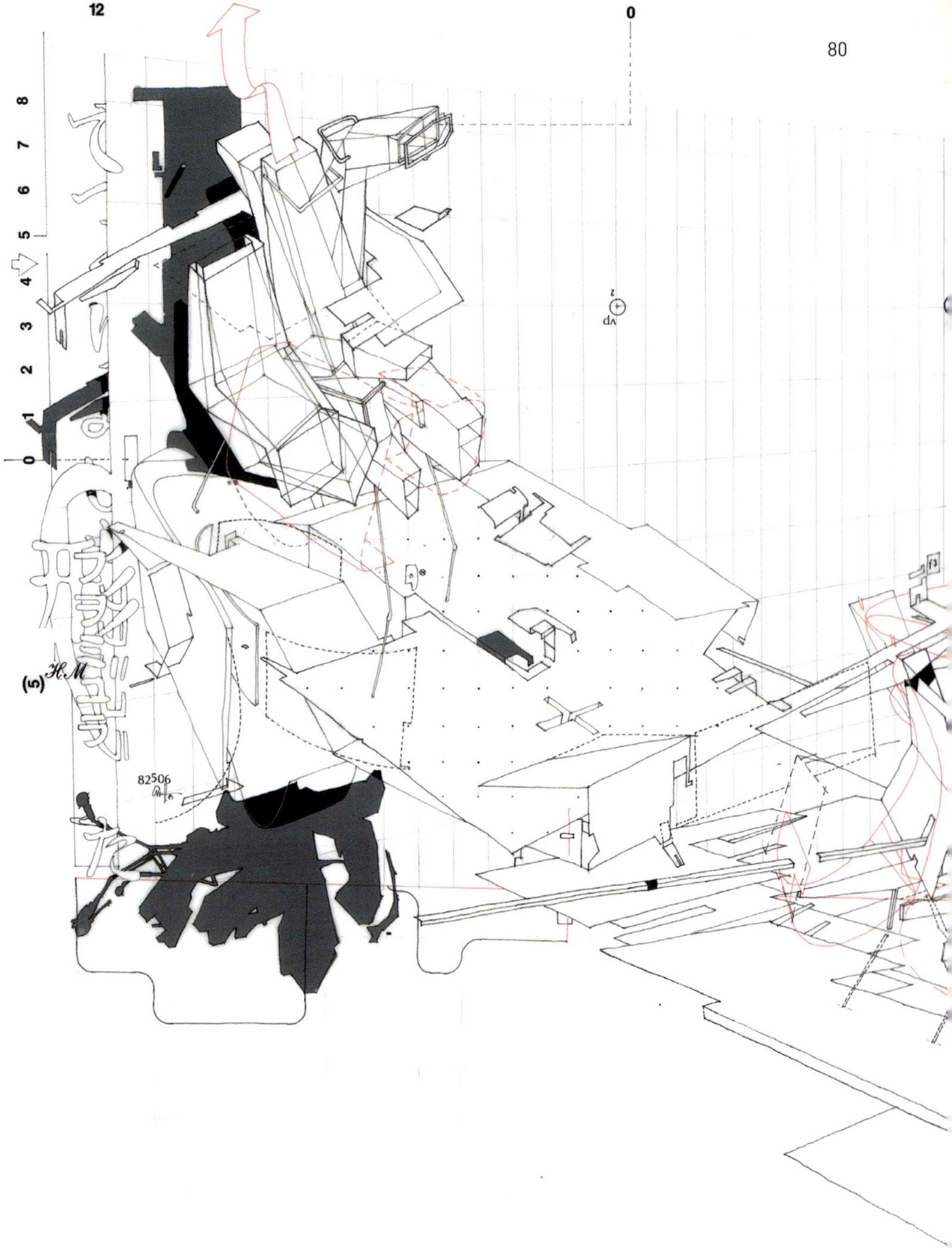

Recognition of the mechanics that make up the act of predrawing – perspectival grids ... construction lines ... crop marks ... and drawing typologies [perspective, elevation, projection, iso ...]

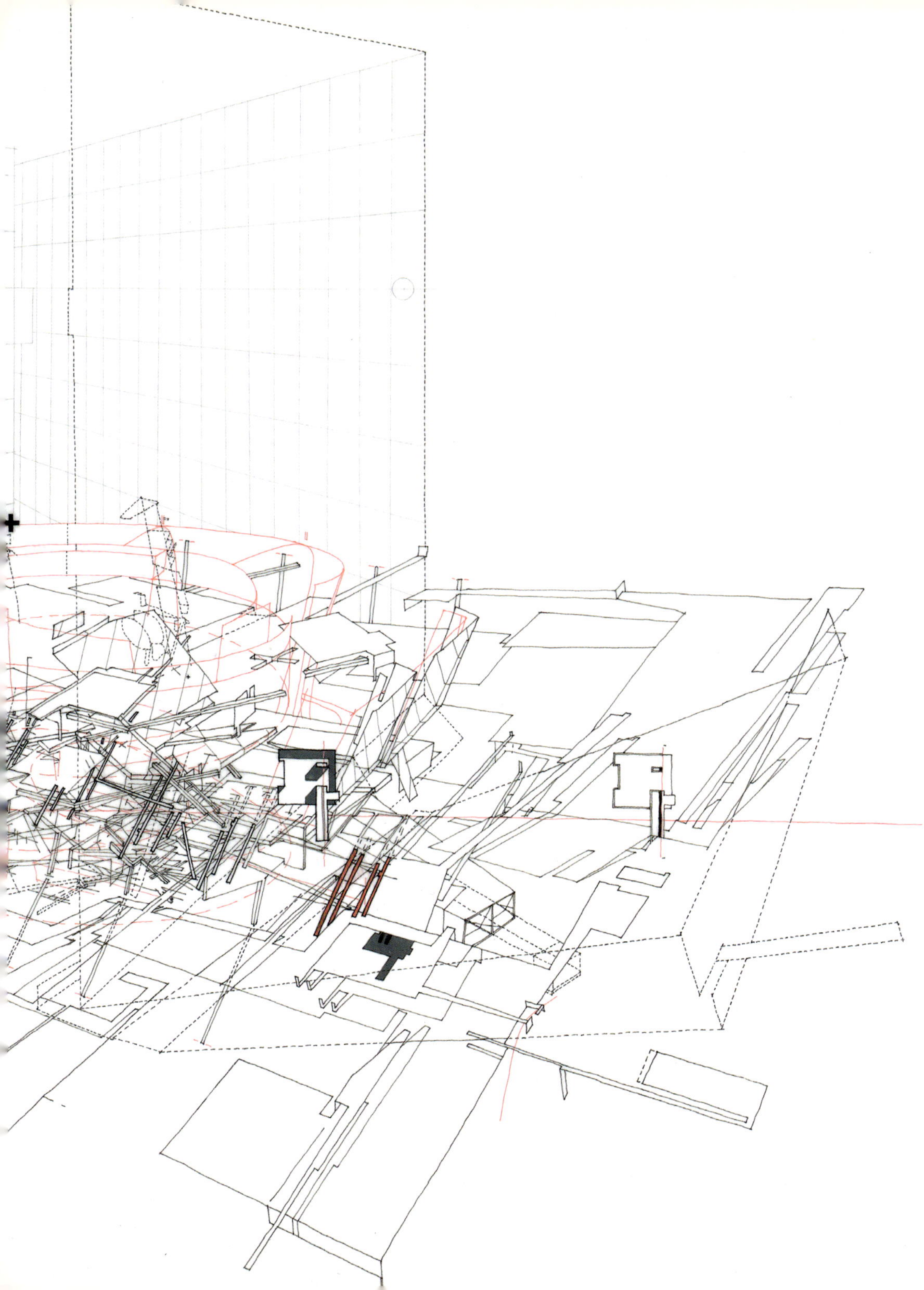

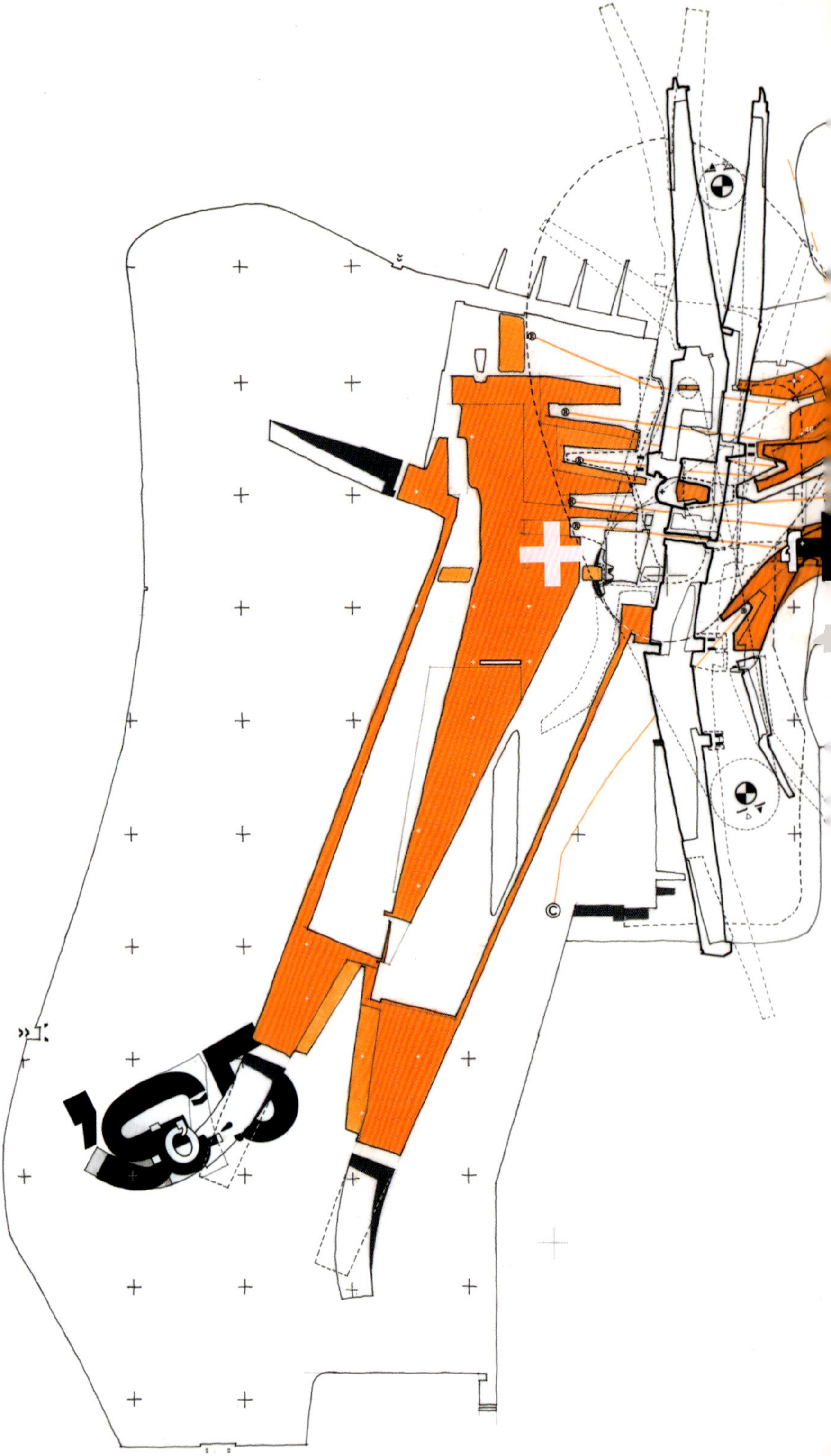

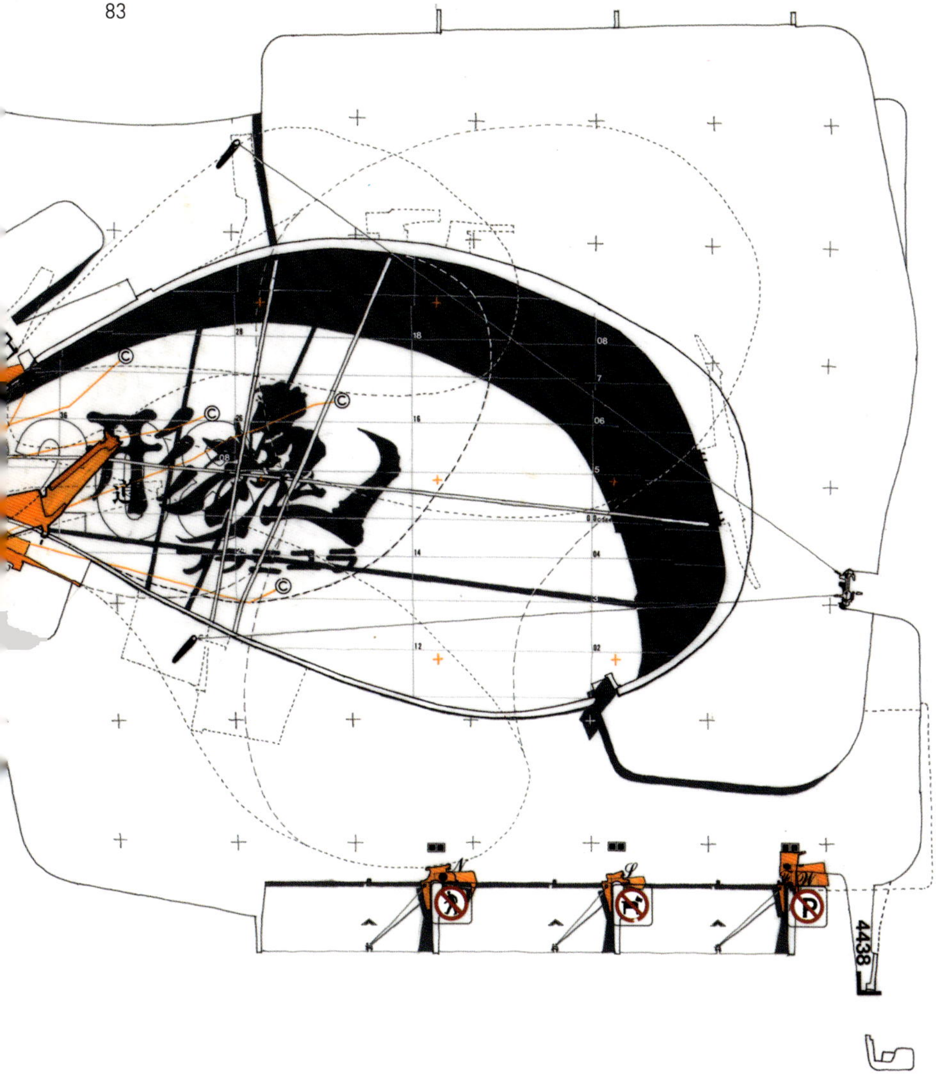
4438

01 EC
ECONOMI[CAL]

Orange County, Southern California.
It seems accidental, but it is not.
It is unrestricted capitalism – the economic equivalent of the Mechudzu.
Strip malls, parking lots, Mediterranean townhomes squeezed together on small lots to imitate Italian density on an unimpeded avenue-highway 2.3 miles from the mall. Dentist offices, chain restaurants, planter pots with toxic palms scattered along sidewalks and space allotments for only certain types of trees.
Homogeneneity in the continuum – acres of development.
Heterogeneity in the eye – miles of stochastic planning. Parking everywhere.
This is the built environment.
The field of stuff.
The stuff on the field.
We are here.

Machinogenesis

Wes Jones & Doug Jackson

As the technical means of drawing – or 2D representation – becomes increasingly sophisticated, the experiential distance between the fantastic and the plausible is reduced. The computer in particular has allowed such representation to become dramatically immersive, engaging viewers in a virtual realm that can be both compellingly real and fantastically free of the physical constraints of everyday reality (as well as the technical constraints of former systems of representation). Yet the work that most effectively exploits these new capabilities is not that which immediately rushes forward to speculate at the furthest reaches of the human imagination, subjecting the viewer to a surreal but ultimately irrelevant phantasmagoria of unimaginable alterity, but rather that which explores more familiar territory, employing the power and freedom of the medium to transform the commonplace into something that is at once unfamiliar but still comprehensible – extending, reshaping, and ultimately critiquing what is currently understood to be real.

The work of Bryan Cantley takes this latter approach, introducing the viewer to a fantastic, speculative otherworld that is anchored in reality. In this *enhanced* reality – spelled out in a wealth of richly detailed drawings and renderings – the familiar is multiplied and transformed through countless permutations into a dizzying, Piranesian version of itself. For Cantley, as for Piranesi, technology is the fabric of reality, and the *machine* is the medium of embodiment. Because of its familiarity, the machine also serves as an exegetical link between everyday reality and the hyperreality he has crafted, transforming itself in the process to ultimately challenge the nature of this familiarity, opening a door to new and unforeseen possibilities.

The relationship between humans and their machines is intimate, and for that reason, complex. This use of the machine as his primary subject lends Cantley's work a particular accessibility, and then an anxious edginess. Machines serve not only as straightforward tools, but also as less innocent symbols of the purposes they embody. For, as embodied intentions or desires, machines bear the hopes, and reveal the fears, that led to their production. In the best cases they have an almost totemic quality, providing a spectacle of mechanical accomplishment that captivates and coheres the society that invents it – and bears witness to it. Machines are inevitably in close physical contact with those who make use of them, serving as extensions of the human body (literally in some cases), magnifying both its capabilities (fostering a sense of closeness and familiarity) and its foibles (which tempers this familiarity with a slight wariness). This intimate relationship has resulted in a generally high level of mechanical literacy in society, apparent in the tendency to anthropomorphize machines and the common use of mechanical metaphors. The installation of technology as a familiar "other" establishes it as both common and exotic, as the most "ready to hand" and, for the same reason, the most ready to harm.

These poignant cultural associations connected to the machine are used by Cantley to draw viewers into his work, and to inflect the experience of the environment his work depicts. The innate closeness to the machine that humans enjoy, evident in its general *legibility*, provides his audience with a means to decode the otherwise overwhelming barrage of mechanical imagery he has created. While the whole image may be incomprehensible, individual moments clearly stand out as familiar and understandable, serving as anchors in the roiling sea of mechanical flotsam, engaging the viewer's attention, and holding out the promise of further comprehension.

Yet the stability of these anchors is illusory: as the viewer is drawn further into Cantley's maelstrom, the innate mechanical literacy that promised comprehension is frustrated. In fact, the environment described by Cantley's images is *not* mechanical in the end, but something entirely other. "Mechanical" denotes function or performance, connoting an engineered economy of means; if mechanical is Kansas, then this is not Kansas. The innumerable struts, stabilizers, linkages, actuators, hydraulic hoses, sissy bars, louvered vents, warning stripes, and monocoque shells – not to mention the graphic elements typically accompanying their representation – that suffuse Cantley's work and clamor for the viewer's attention are, however, not Oz either. In fact, these myriad elements seem incapable of being resolved into any kind of coherent whole, mechanical or fantastic, and likewise impossible to relate to any particular function with which the viewer may be familiar.

The environment of Cantley's work might more appropriately be termed *machinic*, to distinguish it from the merely (or more straightforwardly, or more logically, or more determinedly) mechanical. Whereas the mechanical object stipulates a one-to-one correspondence between itself and a particular function, and between each of its parts and the particular role it performs in fulfilling that function, the machinic environment of Cantley's work breaks down that narrowly particular formation by deconstructing the components of the machine, deobjectifying it, and smearing its bits across the visual space in a not completely hierarchical field. This resulting "machinic space" is devoid of functional organization – its elements are not parts of some logical whole; instead, they seem to exist *a priori*, in a fundamental, ideal state, open to multiple readings and multiple assemblies.

As an example, this conceit of a machinic world is reinforced by the graphic elements that Cantley employs – particularly the *hiragana* and *katakana* Japanese character sets that frequently appear in his images. These graphic devices operate with the same levels of familiarity and exoticism as the mechanical elements, setting up expectations in the viewer that are subtly transformed with greater (though ultimately frustrated) understanding. Since the (Western) viewer is familiar with the ideographic nature of Chinese writing, the implied relationship to the mechanical objects sharing the visual space is expected and satisfying. But just as the mechanical elements are not actually mechanical, so these symbols are not in fact *kanji*. Whereas the ideographic *kanji* characters of Chinese writing form the original basis of the Japanese script, they, like the purely mechanical object, rely on a direct correspondence – in this case between a particular character and an idea: each *kanji* character is derived from a picture of a particular object or concept, and thus its range of signification is narrow. Japanese, however, subsequently developed two syllabic scripts to supplement the borrowed *kanji* characters; these resulting *hiragana* and *katakana* characters are symbols derived from elements of the original *kanji*, with each symbol corresponding only to a particular sound rather than a word or idea. As such, they can be redistributed in multiple ways to arrive at multiple meanings, analogous to the way that the machinic elements in Cantley's drawings, by virtue of their more elemental nature, are capable of supporting multiple readings in contrast to the single reading typically afforded by the mechanical object.

This Japanese text, in combination with the gridlines, axes, arrows, registration marks, and other graphic symbols common to mechanical delineation, are teasingly used by Cantley to ostensibly clarify his work, while simultaneously acting as visual chaff, and serve as countermeasures to intelligibility. Even their nature as aloof, neutral graphic symbols is called into question, as they occasionally exhibit a physical status equivalent to the elements they overlay, interacting with them, casting and receiving shadows, and providing a degree of obfuscation that keeps the field of possibility from resolving itself too easily into a singular, limited reading.

These tactics for delaying – or just denying – comprehension maintain an openness that allows for the liberation of possibilities latent within the machine, but which otherwise remain currently unrecognized. The machine is typically regarded as an irreducible object narrowly defined by its particular function, for example, a limited human construct contrasted with the unlimited possibility of nature. In Cantley's machinic world, on the other hand, the machine is deobjectified and reconstituted as the very fabric of the environment itself, becoming, therefore, a kind of alternate nature, burgeoning with unlimited potential. Considered this way, Cantley's take on the machinic can be understood as the genetic basis of this new environment, the raw material from which are derived not only the more familiar linkages, frames, hoses, and graphic quasi-objects that populate Cantley's images, but also a menagerie of new elements – articulated Boolean aggregates, locally massive or attenuated, smooth or crystalline – an evolutionary explosion of new and hybrid species born out of a primordial machinic soup, formally and logically congruent with, but nevertheless distinct from, the machine as it is currently conceived.

As a generator of novel architectural form, of course, this version of the machinic is only one of many, and must compete for attention these days with the more fashionable and copious output of blobs and other

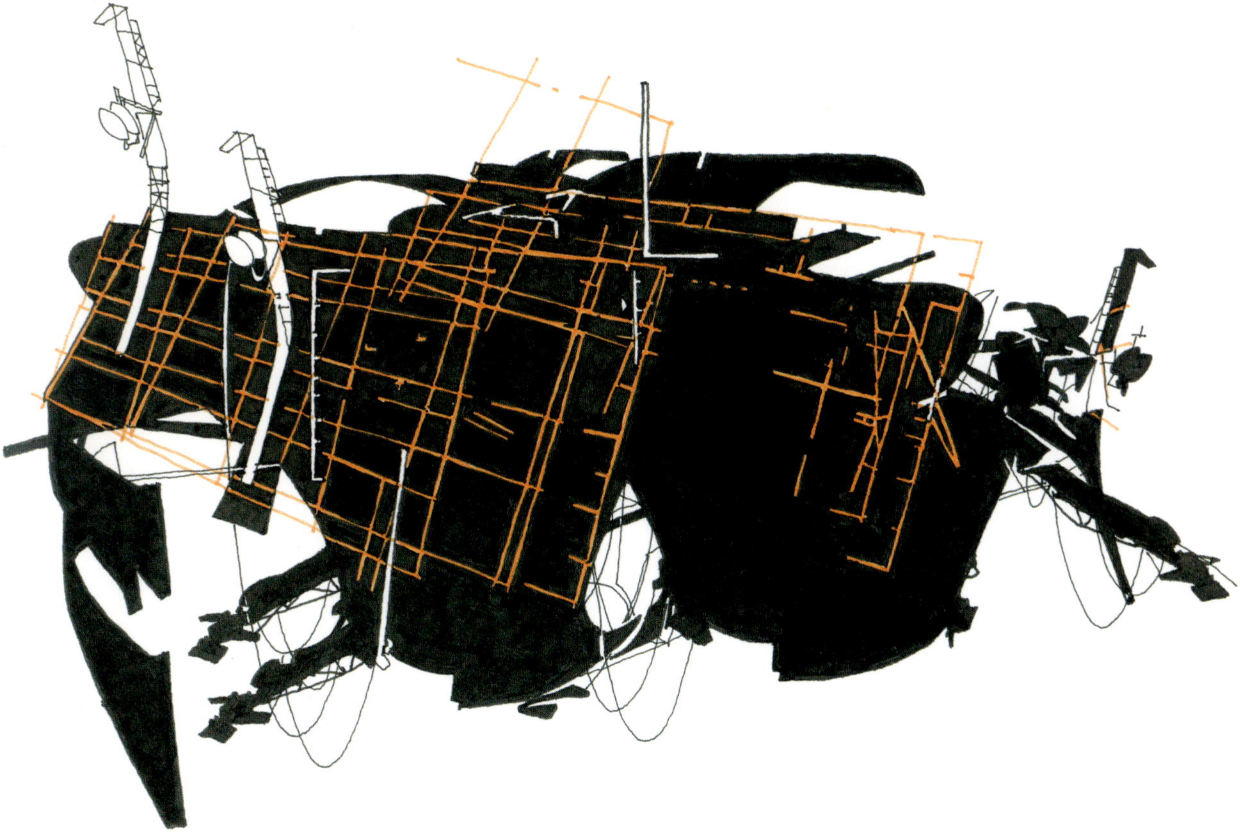

curiosities spawned by software borrowed from Hollywood. However, given the machinic's provenance in the mechanical, and the richness and depth of the relationship between humans and their mechanical constructs, the novel form generated from Cantley's machinic field of possibility distinguishes itself from the blob's more shallow efforts by virtue of its inheritance of the machine's familiar logic and natural ability to engage – qualities which are notably absent from the inscrutable, aloof, and ardently alien blob: its invocation of a biomorphic connection notwithstanding, the blob primarily capitalizes on its shock value, asserting its outright difference as its basis of valuation and thereby captivating the viewer only in the manner of a freak-show attraction.

In contrast, the machinic offers the possibility of novel form that is both captivating and engagingly familiar, form that, while pre-functional, can suggest functionality, or otherwise demonstrate the means of its integration into the outside world. And, while the abstract realm of Cantley's images remains, like the blob, unconstrained by such issues as gravity, durability, function, and economy, his machinic formalism nevertheless acknowledges the important role that these real world limitations play in the framing and evaluation of Architecture. Consequently, in the absence of such constraints, it adopts an elective restraint, hewing closely to the established way that humans have always constructed their relationship to the world as already embodied in their machines. This lends its novelty a distinct credibility, and offers a viable means for its graduation from the arena of representation and its ultimate realization in the everyday world, where it might stand judgment as Architecture.

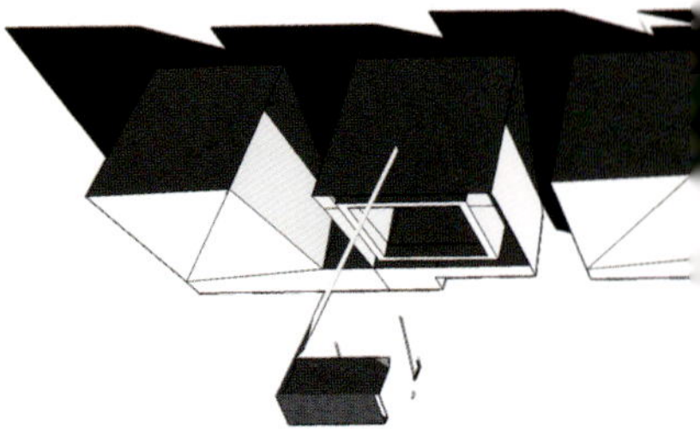

Housing Prototype NH02

This is not a project that attempts to solve the antisocial issues of **privacy-branding** within the urban context. It assumes privacy is desired and that the sense of privacy protection is heightened with the unknown passersby. It accepts its role as a social informant, a receptacle for the present condition of privacy control.

The "**antiwelcome mat**" suggests a condition that dwellers do not offer their home as an open condition – they do so only upon identification and invitation.

There is a blurring of the identity of "figure" to "ground," where *surface behavior* becomes a qualifying description more than *location* or *orientation*. It acknowledges the "corridor effect" – the "walls" of the generic fabric *eventspace* of the repetitive grid of blocks. **NH02** continues the gesture with its monolithic street membrane. The slight breaks or moments of view that occur within the facade membrane are reflections of the patterns inherent in the ground level of most of the city, moments of pause that occur within the urban matrix – traffic lights, saying hello. The edge of the street; the sidewalk; the fence; the gate; the front yard; the facade; the front door ... these are all symbolic layers that address issues of the transition or the segregation of public into private.

NH02 explores the very basic idea of the function of a wall itself – to separate and to classify possibility and purpose *on either side*.

Please come in?

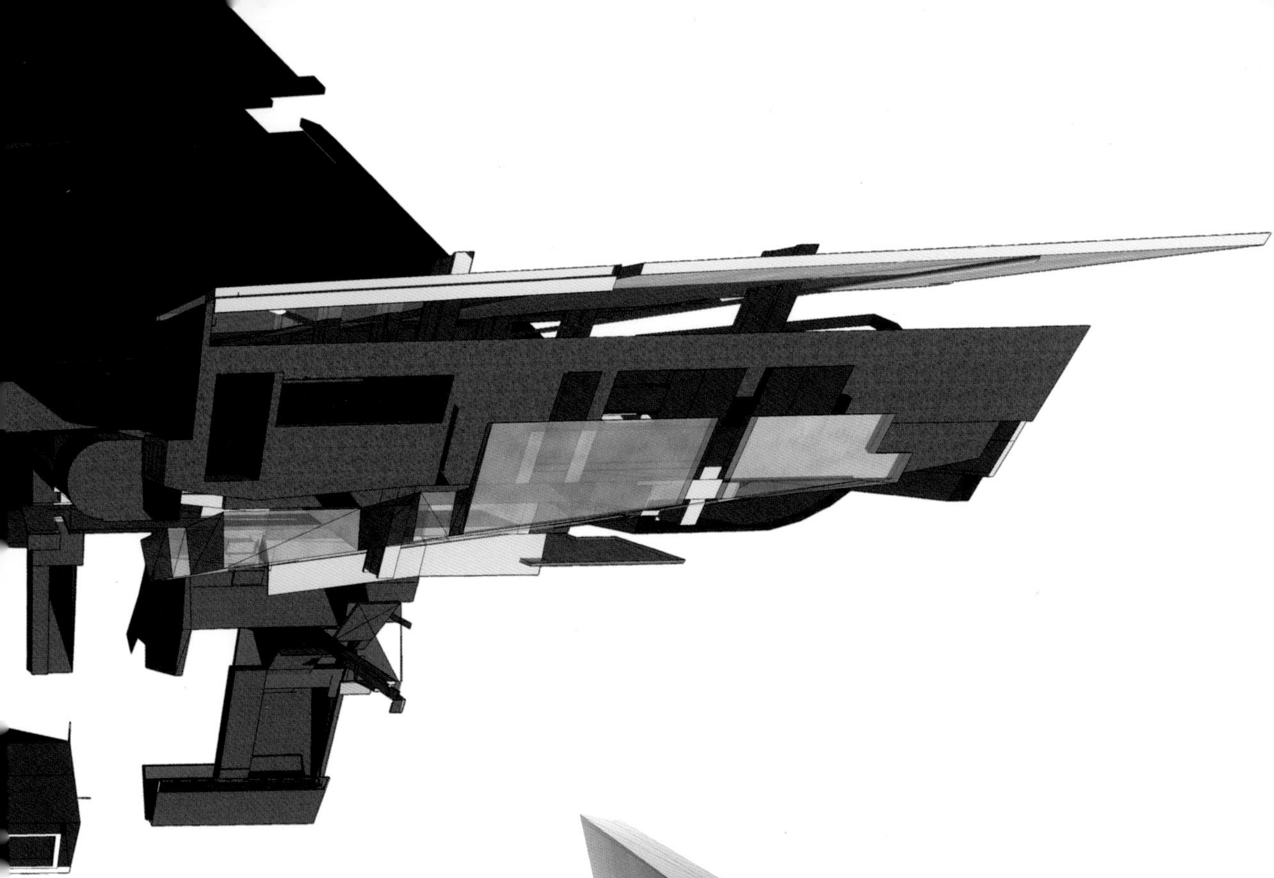

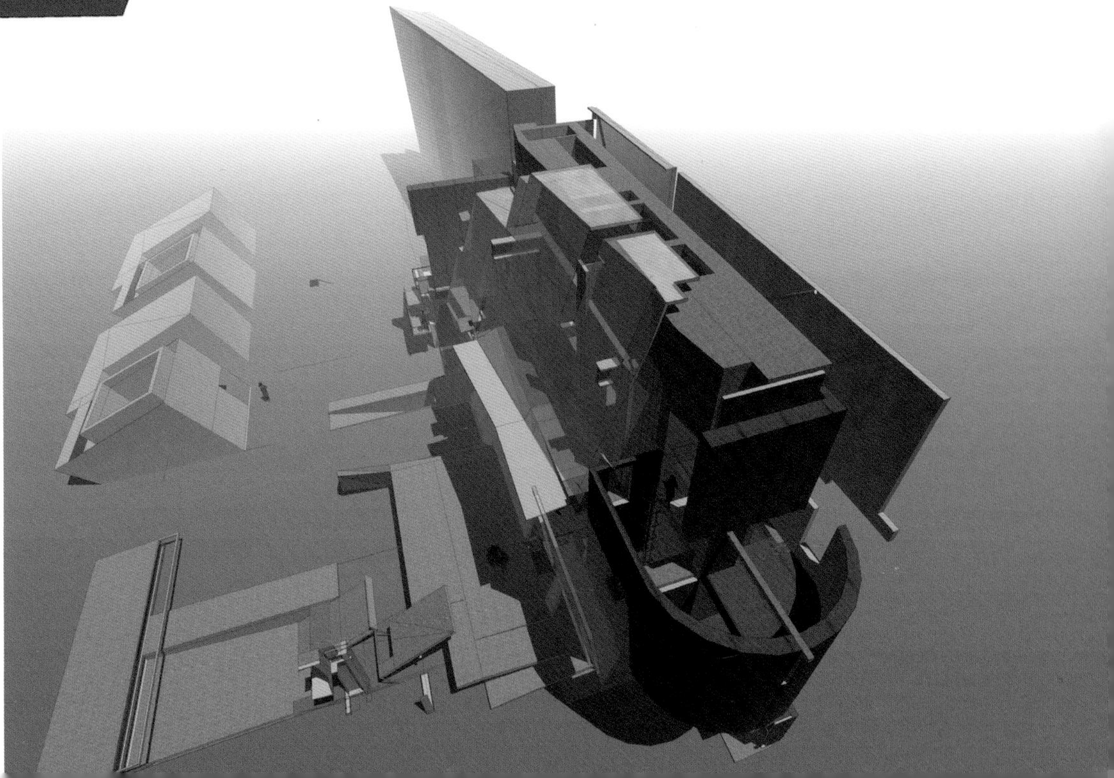

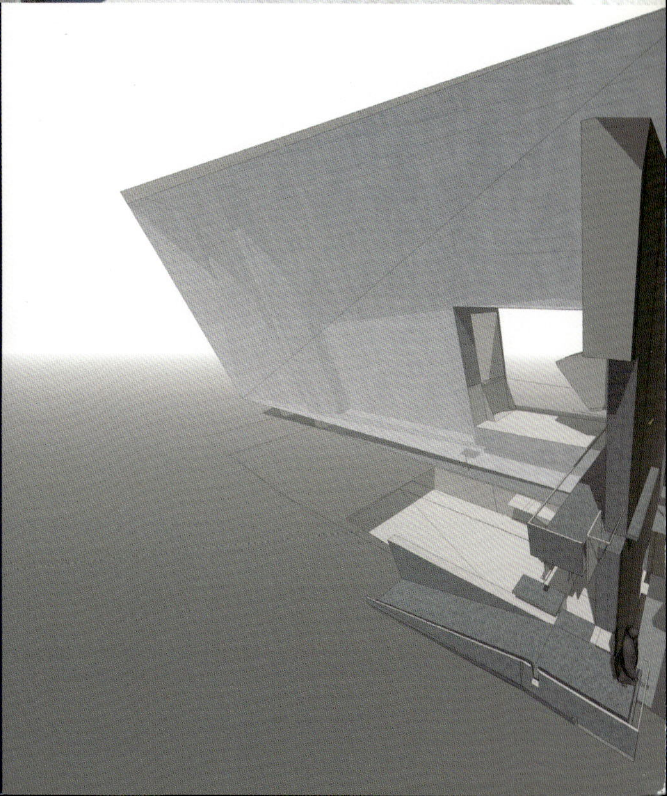

Domestic imprinting. The documentation of the transitions from inclusive to exclusive. The house as a drawing surface. The home as a Xerox machine for living [jacked into the mainframe].

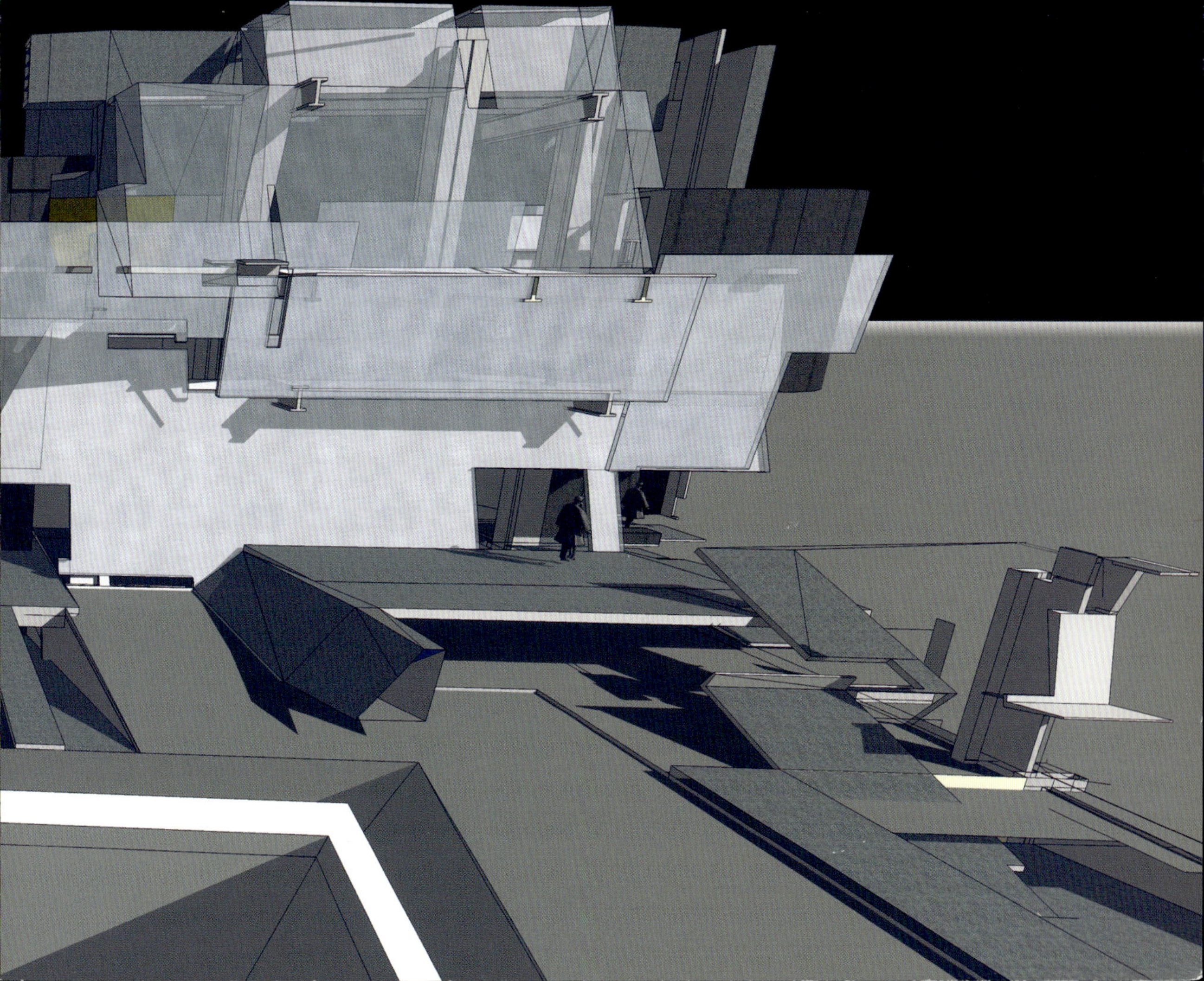

X.Com

X.Com was an advertising agency in Santa Ana, Ca., the first professional occupant of the then newly dubbed Artists' Village. As a small 7-person firm, X.Com was considered one of the most cutting-edge ad agencies in Orange County. The budget was small, the site even smaller, and the program, as befitting a new and gritty office, was odd – an INTERNAL fire egress stair, a restroom entry on a landing vestibule, and large steel gates that could be locked down, while still allowing access through the space.

As our first commission in the OC, Form:uLA was similarly a new office, and our agility with this project represented a threshold moment for us. X.Com was the birthplace of Mechudzu. By observing the constant give-and-take of the design/build scenario, the ebb and flow with the contractor, the client, and the site during construction, we began to envision the theoretical possibilities of immersive and constant responsiveness. Like the call and response of jazz, we envisioned the process as an organic composite of mechanical pieces ... of detail components ... and programmatic "shifting". For every move, there were a myriad of responses [information] ... each of which then recycled back and altered the original cast [deformation]. This oscillation took place in real time. It was a breathing entity, becoming one with the process of establishing a biological pattern of invasion and resuscitation. Mechudzu.

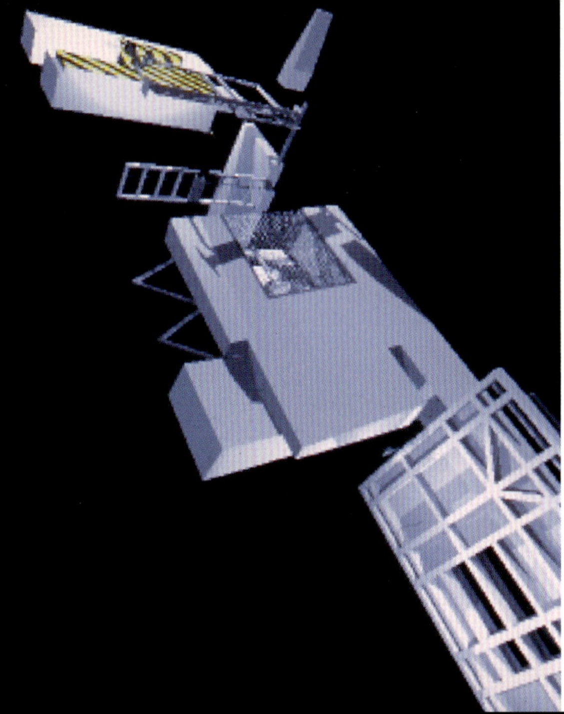

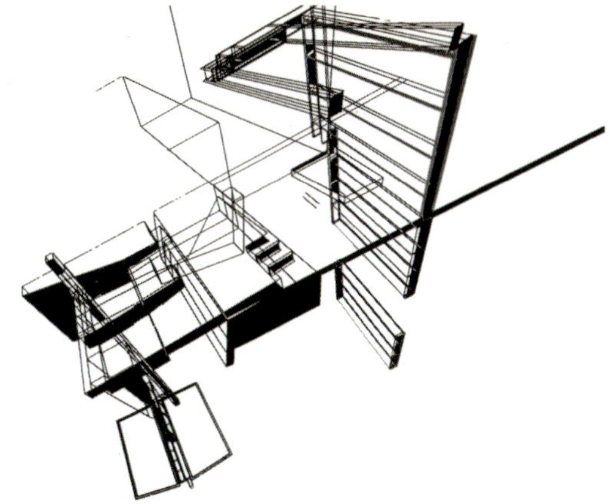

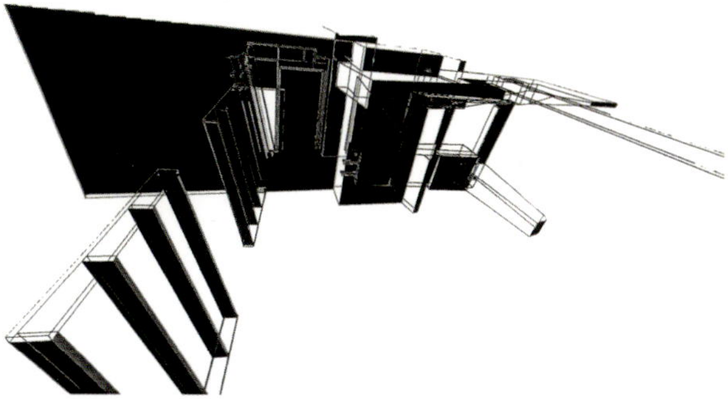

The emergence of the "surfacescape" as an intelligent membrane began with X.Com circa 1995. The first exploration of the veneer of Orange County.

TnA [Truth and Advertising]

"The architectural drawing as an end work can ***function*** *in any of three ways: as an innovative design tool; as the articulation of a new direction; or as a creation of consummate artistic merit.*
Put simply, a ***perfect act of architecture*** *achieves all three at once."* – Terence Riley

This project is for a 4000sf advertising agency in Santa Ana, California. The final composition resulted from observations from Digital Paper® drawings and a corresponding understanding of surface-space relationships.

Certain regions of the project were developed around the notion of constructing the Artificial Simultane, to provide an environment that seems to be many places at once. The client proposed two simultaneous ideas regarding spatial identity. The first concept was what he described as a "water cooler effect," or a central gathering space, where informal collisions and conversations would spark the creative resources and personalities within his ad agency. The second idea was to create an artificial urban landscape, or a series of urban objects tied together based on locations, interactions, and collisions, but which also were allowed to have their own identity within a hypothetical cityscape.

The main design studio was conceived as a fractured translucent box within a box within a box, and later dubbed the "Ice Cave." Its purpose was twofold: first, to shield the computer users from the wall of natural light along the west street elevation; second, to allow that natural light to filter into the rest of the spaces, for the benefit of those who did not need such restrictive light requirements.

Program and space planning dictated the location of the "dark zones" of computer studios to be located near the now unshielded windows. We took the challenge of this duality of program to create a condition of simultaneity; becoming both a screen as well as a transmission device – it prevents transmission on one level, and allows it on another. From a conceptual standpoint, this translucent series of envelopes also became a device that allows many views at one time. We wanted the spatial disruption to serve as a datum to tie the harder components together through a distortion of view. The ice cave, with its inherent chaos of distorted multiple vantage points, became, if you will, the energy, passion, and confusion of the flux of motion in the hive mentality of the modern city. Take away the swarm of connective tissue from the grid and we have left only isolated monoliths.

TnA explores the generation of a creative studio space using the tablet as a generating device. All design decisions, development, and documentation, including some of the construction documents, were performed on tablet computers. The entire project was designed using SketchUp, a relatively low-end modeling program when compared with the hypercomplexities of Maya, Form-Z, or Rhino. This program was chosen because of the fluidity and almost elementary simplicity of its interface. We literally "drew" the project in the third dimension, as opposed to purely modeling it in a digital format.

A design chronology using the tablet unfolded as such:

Phase 1: Survey of the Space
We took possession of the raw shell ... taking dimensions, digital images, and confirming the actual site conditions with the existing drawings. The drawings rarely matched the building as it was actually constructed. Drawings tell us a lot, even going as far as legal documentation, but they are never an "exact" condition. So the digital files of our survey were used as "as-builts." After the tablet survey was complete, we walked the site, the "as-builts" confirmed *"what was drawn"* with *"what was built."*

Phase 2: Site Gestures
We developed a technique of taking snapshots at the site using the tablets (then an absurd proposal). We drew directly on top of the snapshots using Photoshop to suggest zoning, massing, or space allotment.

Phase 3: On-site Meetings
We would have weekly construction meetings with the client and contractor at the job site to talk about the design IN THE SPACE. We could pull up sketches and models while on-site, thus talking about "real-time" design potentials and conditions. This alleviated a lot of initial confusion about "where did *this* go?" and "what did *that* look like?"

Phase 4: Revisions *
Meetings with client and contractor were held often to discuss revisions in the design, both in terms of editing design elements, as well as confronting anomalies in the construction process. In this case, the "as-builts" were crucial documents. We could handle an issue on real time pull up the digital model, make suggestions and changes, have the client and the contractor approve the changes with a cost estimate, and email the changes to each party BEFORE we even left the spot. This was done in premobile computing 2004.

Phase 5: Clothing
During construction, and more specifically the framing phase, we were able to "skin" elements in Photoshop at the site to show the client what the space would begin to look like. This was sort of an extra service that made the client feel at ease when looking at the jungle of exposed studs.

Phase 6: Construction Details
Here, we used the tablet on site-to compare the digital model with the final construction to further address the common issues of building. When odd conditions came up, were able to walk the space with the contractor and show him the digital model on-site to let him know which parts he would have to alter at HIS cost. *The client LOVED this part of the process.*

The drawing surface leaving its mark on the marking device. The reverse Directional. This is what happens when the page draws back ...

The flux of an interaction, the infinite number of spatial relationships, the dances between workers and work objects that occur on a daily basis were used to make distinctions in the space. The interaction of body, space, and site were critical in the client's mind to make harmony of an otherwise chaotic, passionate work environment. This became an opportunity to implement ideas that we had generated in virtual worlds, such as conceptual eventspaces that occur simultaneously. In other words, we began to conceive the project as we did our drawings.

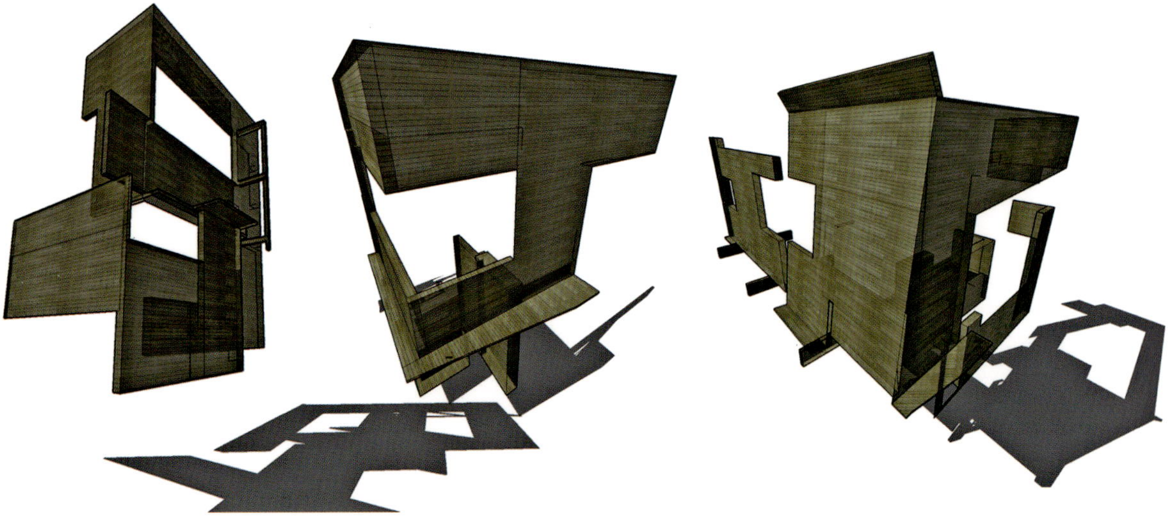

San Clemente CON-do RE:*surf*Face

Overlooking a bluff in San Clemente, the condo complex was a typical 1980s' bland, overcooked soup. The client requested that the condo be re-skinned in such a way as to remove the dry rot and water damage to the existing stucco facade; the new skin assist in the prevention of further damage; and the condo be given a stylistic "upgrade."

"Our main contact related that the group of four owners had expressed an interest in also adding to the resale value – their hope was that by addinng a more interesting facade, the project would speak to the context of the local artistic beach community.

Our response was to develop an engineered slat wall system that would resist weathering, while at the same time allow slivers of light into a *limbotic* cavity buffering the structures. Our concept was to establish a continuous skin that would serve a multifunctional scenario – it would at the same time serve as balcony separators, shade devices, entry node designators, vertical circulation delineators, trash area screening, and program indicators.

The skin system also reconfigured the illusion of the block massing of the two-building/five-unit arrangement. Openings were used to reassign the standard value of logically placed windows in an unexpected way. Subtle shifts in geometries were used to alter the orientation of the original configuration.

The membranes were placed off the actual building facade, promoting a zone of separation where the occupant and visitor would be able to observe the conflict of geometries. This space of filtered light, and the augmented, shaped shadow became a new visual area for the condo community.

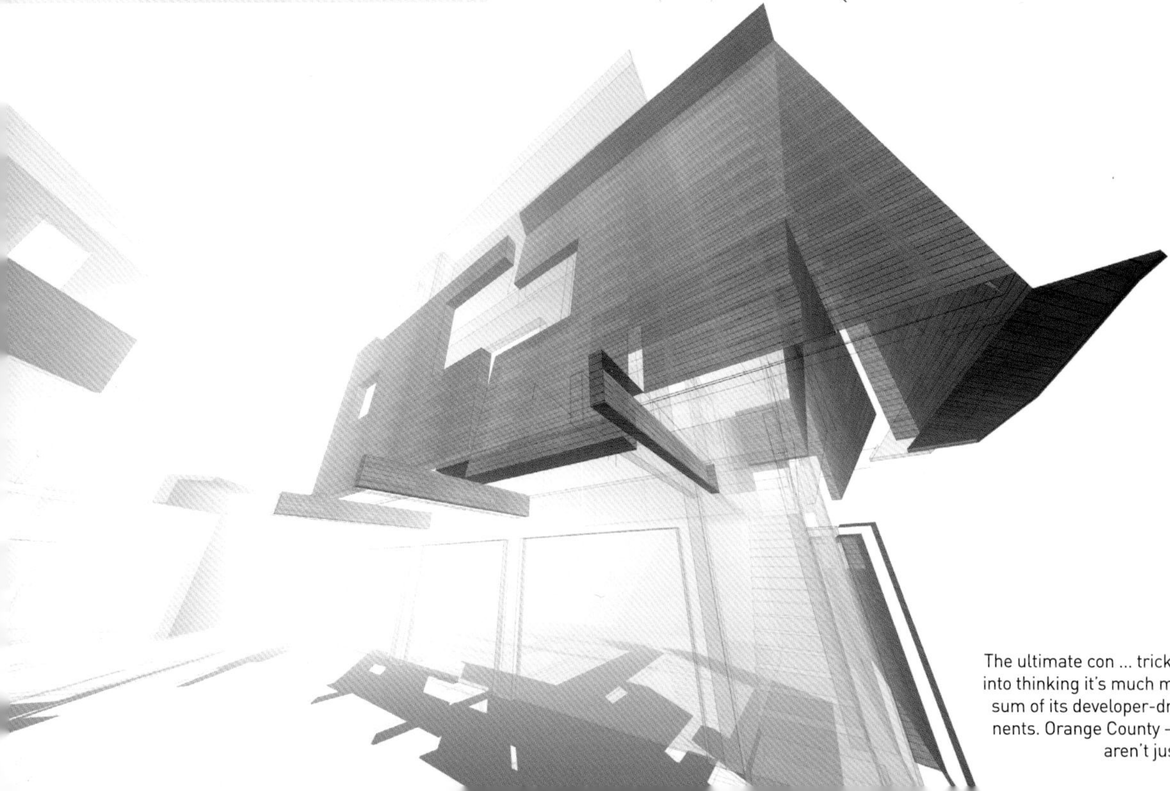

The ultimate con ... trick the building into thinking it's much more than the sum of its developer-driven components. Orange County – the facelifts aren't just skin-deep.

Santa Ana Monument Sign

Client: Truth and Advertising / City of Santa Ana, CA

The client expressed a desire to subvert the typical "monument signage" for city entry points – the standard, traditional facade that displays emblems of the city's various civic organizations [Kiwanis, Shriner, etc.]. TnA wanted a "graphic intervention," which became an object of wonderment, as opposed to a mere backdrop.

The solution was the idea of a single, folded membrane, perforated to reduce wind forces at the site. The graphic labeling was requested by the client to suggest that Santa Ana could "keep up" with the rest of the world in terms of architectural language. Hydraulic pistons extend to leveler arms to adjust the angle of reception on the sloped site adjacent to the freeway entry. Variations of the sign would be generated throughout the city.

This project represents the convergence of the graphic and theoretical layering on top of the economical more directly than any of the current built work.

The panel is the sheet is the drawing is the theory is the stratum. It's everything Orange County has to offer ... and less! Which side of the Curtain are *you* on?

oOAL

AL.chemi[cal]

The Typo in the Topo

The Politics of a Utopian Veneer

Bryan Cantley / Form:uLA

Your computer has insufficient memory to run this program ...
Defrag disk.

The hacker. In this time of reform ... of political correctness ... of desensitization through media saturation ... Why speak of the nature of conflict? Why think about examining the fringes/causes/results of the error message, instead of working to run error-free? It's important to understand that I am not talking of conflict in terms of resolving it – I'm speaking of simply acknowledging it. Conflict occurs when two or more systems are *seemingly* incompatible. The benign and the malignant. The conservative versus the liberal. Problem-solving versus inquiry. Or, in the *Act* of Architecture – drawing versus building ...

There exists a condition of misrepresentation within the guise of the "architectural drawing" that informs the condition of Experimental Architecture, one that is born from, and celebrates, the notion of conflict. Perhaps it attempts to unify; perhaps it resonates with the idea of propagating the turmoil; it fluctuates between the two extremes, allowing the observer/inhabitant/occupant to formulate and reformulate the idea of "resolution" in an ongoing, uncertain manner – much like we dwell in the uncertainty and chaos in the condition of life. Drawing, following its definition, is a membrane of suggestive information. The category of drawing, in this book, additionally serves as a membrane of suggestive connectivity and fragmentation. It serves to be a threshold between what we think is "real" architecture and what we imagine is "experimental" architecture.

My work attempts to illustrate without rectification, observing the situational position of "conflict" – no attempt either to pass judgment, or to propose a *solution*. There is only suggestive information.

Welcome to Myopia
The Suppression of ExperiMental Architecture [Behind the Orange Curtain]

In the past I had resisted the notion that architecture is a political act. Or, that it was anything but what I might label as a "surface" act, in that I had always insisted that it was a formal exercise over anything else. But over the last twenty years of living in, looking at, and "practicing" in Orange County [the "OC"], I must admit to my rampant case of myopia. Architecture, in *this* social environment, is indeed political. The argument against the form has become more important than the form itself. I describe the conditions behind the "Orange Curtain" to suggest that experimental architecture, and its investigative and nonlinear thinking, is, in this world, shunned as petty. Insignificant. The generic guard is impenetrable. And from its fortress, I use the microcosm of the OC to call out the conflictive nature of injecting the experimental into an unwilling, or at least uneducated subject. The operating system must allow the program to be installed according to its parameters. *Cannot read path/filename; unknown file format* is becoming more and more an expected response.

I have seen this response often – groups and individuals rise with fervor to *that which is without passion and substance.* An artifical environment of artifical rules. The endless installation and removal of thousands of programs on your hard drive. The end result: fragmentation and loss of *freshspace* [where experiments flourish] is incredible.

There is an ever-present entity of what might be described as layering in Orange County driven chiefly by economy and trade. These layers may be described geologically as "strata," although they appear more as information. At the bottom, there takes place a stratum of building that is composed of a vast number of hardened and present layers of what may best be described as **"noncritical" information**. *Bloatware. Creeping Featuritis.* Most of this information is *political.* Not in terms of boundaries and parties, but more in terms of unwritten policy and governing systems. This should entail an architectural response – but even the local architectural profession might be implicated here.

This network, this layering of noncritical political envelopes has created a distinguished new fabric in the OC, and in much of the educated world. Indeed, there has been so much of policy for policy's sake that the nature of the profession has asphyxiated, and is struggling to breathe any of the unsullied air dissipating near a distant surface ... or perhaps is buried under the myriad of trivial layers that have been shoveled on by the sociopolitical machine. This new type of surface is multidimensional, insomuch as it occupies both the "x" and "y" zones of the geographical and financial boundaries of the county [i.e. the birth of the all-too-sobering term "The Orange Curtain"], as well as the social, intellectual, and critical "z" axis of *idea.* This is a rich material composed of decades upon decades of repression and *facade* – it has become almost impenetrable, as the creators and keepers would have it. Justification, if not celebration, of the nature of the mundane, the benign, the layers of numbness.

Formally, it is quite an impressive membrane, nourished by orthodoxy, shaped by homogeneity, and thick in its apathy. If ever there was an "old boys' network", it's thriving in geocentric safe pockets across the globe.

Playing ever so softly in the background, like your operating system simply *being there*, silently governing the processes and programs that you attempt to manipulate on a daily basis. Ultimately, a typical player may only do what the operating systems *allows* it to do. The power lies with the programmer.

I see this *layering*, the very source of the numbing disempowerment, as precisely the place for intervention, for experimentation, for mechudzu to take root and spread. Chris Gray, in *The Cyborg Handbook*, states that there have been three major directions that have shaped the study of cyborgology. The first are the *Mechanists* – or those who pursue actual physical augmentation of existing bodies focusing on the EXTERNAL, representing the present; second, the *Shapers* – those who induce technology at the root structure level through DNA, thus altering from the INTERNAL, initiating change at the molecular level, and representing the future; and third, the *Lobsters* – those who combine approaches, suspending their physical entities in artificial, man-made "shells" or membranes, and reside in the esoteric and constructed realms of *nonplace* [cyberspace]. The condition of change lies somewhere between realms of the *Shapers* and the *Lobsters*. If we propose a reweaving of the layers, and restratification of the information, then we have an opportunity to avoid a situation of becoming appliqué.

If there exists a vast surface that runs as deep as it does wide, protected by the communal thought and policy it protects, then the form precipitates the very elitist walls of this "utopia." *This surface needs to change. It needs to breathe.* We need to shed the orange-colored glasses and begin to examine our own input into this topological phenomenon.

My hypothesis is that a stagnation has prevented any "rippling" of the surface of the OC, and of the conservative climate overall. Every so often, without any regularity, new conjecture comes along that precipitates a slight misalignment of the data that makes up that surface. *A rogue code. Malware.* When that idea is allowed voice, a ripple occurs in the hybrid surface. Throw the smallest grain into a still pond ... a ripple occurs. This ripple marks an obscure event in the outer shell. Most often the repression comes up from within to smooth it back out. Even if there is a condition of permanence, it is so small in comparison to the entity that it is quickly lost in the vastness of scale. Or it becomes a simple enough exercise to calmly and quietly add more noncritical layers in the form of jargon or policy to hide it away between the strata, literally smothering it, concealing it from the ever-present danger of curious eyes. It's a VERY impressive media machine. It's a very contagious space, this layer of smooth persuasiveness. But it's not perfect.

ExperiMental Architectural events are quickly surrounded and choked by normal *thinking*. Covering up an event with *other* information does not deny the event – it simply attempts to remove it from the conversation, again with volumes of noncritical data. Enter the political machine. Let the rogue idea be denied by refusing it acknowledgment. Overwrite the drive with enough binary code, and then the hiccup goes unnoticed.

Herein lies the conflict within the very nature of ExperiMental Architecture. The environments and communities in which it is most needed, the benign, the uninformed, are the very ones that seem to attempt to violently dispel the organism from the host. *The application has stopped working. Restart your computer.* The Curtain it seems has an egress mechanism, a sole point of willing penetration. Perhaps the path of expulsion is the means to inhabit the membrane, thus becoming integral structurally to the defensive membrane. Be a layer.

Layering is not easy, it takes patience. *iTunes was not installed properly. Please reinstall iTunes.* It craves *"sameness"* [*copy, paste*], it is always a challenge of recognizing the crippling effect of the *layer-ization*. One ripple is not enough. There must be enough ripples, scars, folds, and warps to permanently become part *of* the very fabric which attempts a cerebral annihilation. The structure of scar tissue behaves as a much stronger, more resistive entity than the original material. It is formed after a rupture, in an attempt to mend the altered mesh. Being the cause of the anomaly, as well as the healing component that reinforces the idea, leads most often to *system failure* – a systemic error that requires a cultural *reboot* and the reinstalling of a myriad of positional foci. The ghost in the machine. The face of the *Terminal Command*.

If enough tissue is altered, if enough ripples occur simultaneously, if enough buildup happens near the same schism, ExperiMental Architecture in fact will have become the nonoverlooked component of the intellectual, physical, and architectural -*scapes*. The uprising needn't worry about the attempts to downplay the event – those will always be there, in far greater numbers and with greater resistance than any have the power to overcome. The benign shall rule the state of apathy. Many battles have been fought and lost to promote a true investigative architectural culture – locally and globally. ExperiMental Architecture needs to be revealed to ourselves in great[er] numbers, in as many scenarios as possible. The system needs to be infiltrated, becoming part of the configuration dislodgement.

Consider this is a call to arms. *An opportunity to* ***not*** *download that anti-malware program.*

"This is the way the world ends
Not with a bang but a whimper."
The Hollow Men, T. S. Eliot

* * * * *

The Typo in the Topo ...
Typography ... topography ... typology ...

There is a bike path that I frequent – it provides a situation that perhaps encompasses several of the ideas behind the cataloguing of ExperiMental Architectures. The road surface cracks from external pressures. *Input.* Workers are given direction to "fill the crack" by applying a tar patch over a disruption of the surface – a health and safety issue for bikers. *Process.* The workers, either in an attempt to quickly finish the job, or because the medium in which they are working is somewhat *uncontrollable*, make broad gestures that attempted to comply with the path of the fissures. The result, however, is anything but perfect. *Save.* They at times fill the fissure; at others they miss the mark completely. Sometimes they didn't reach far enough, and at yet other times they overshot their mark considerably. *Print.* Perhaps the most visually interesting of these errant conditions are the places of transitions – either between cracks that are several feet apart [I imagine them slinging the patch material in as few brushstrokes as possible], or where they apparently trailed off the repair, moving on to investigate another disruption, or perhaps to take lunch. Regardless, the events that these strokes make on the canvas of the asphalt are beautiful in their own formal right. They remind me of ancient, masterful Asian brushstrokes in their fluidity, variation of line weight, and denotation of the "hand."

The question is that even though they are not intentional [in the sense of "beauty," but are intentional in the sense of a solution to a problem], are they not still beautiful in their accidental nature? Do they not hold information regarding chronology, intent, critical thinking, strategy, and traces of their human creators [*wabi*]? Are they not transmitters of ideas about translation, interference, juxtaposition, and alternative resolution? Are they in fact NONresolute? *Run Spellcheck.*

These patches are made in an "attempt" to repair a fault: intention versus precision, anomalies embedded within the operating kernel. ExperiMental Architectures may attempt to evoke a similar condition. Perhaps the problems that are attempted at being solved through "traditional" architecture and conservative political organizations may not be the problems needing to be solved. Perhaps we are asking the wrong questions, or at least attempting to solve ones that have been solved time and time again, to the point that the questions themselves no longer require the gestation of an "idea" in order to come to fruition. *Cut. Paste. Copy. Paste ...*

Layers. Patches. Lobsters. I return to the problem of the architectural drawing – a place for experiment, the place of unresolved architecture – architecture for which there can be no leading questions. There is a quickness and impermanence that lends itself to the rapid overlay and thus infection of information, ideas, and trials. A drawing is an impregnated sheet, an inscribed surface membrane. On a paved road, the lines and shapes drawn *in plan* on paper are transposed literally from working drawing to application, from ink to paint. Graphics on paper translate into graphics on the ground – the road is our attempt to create such a flat membrane on which we inscribe line and shape, via the application of solid + dashed lines with other graphic information. Lines, numbers, and other 2-dimensional delineators are transmitted to the ground plane, since in this instance graphic information is about shape [specific information], rather than the origin or terminus of a 3-dimensional system [the edge of a shaped mass]. Therefore, breaks in the pavement [or system], anomalies in the line work that define lanes, and operational procedure based on established rules [*"right lane must turn right"*] graphic intrusions – both intentional and accidental – onto the drawing surface of the road are all examples of the investigative and repositional nature of experimental architectures.

Problems do arise in terms of fostering experimentation when a governing system, a rule-based configuration suppresses the nature to investigate. But here, the very nature of experimentation is marbled with the opportunity, if not expectation, that *things will fail*. Failure of the road is what generated the asphalt anomalies. This has no value to the power regime of systematic control. Anomalies in the system refute the very nature of "control." Pavement patches, and by definition, ExperiMental Architectures, end up *"being"* – an intention to address a "real" set of issues, but with the license and nature to go off path, to become their own conditions. Even in a "real" attempt to solve a problem, i.e. filling in a fissure, a situational intent allows for the potential situation of the uncomfortable, the unrecognizable.

New datasets are formed from the observation of the breakdown of accepted norms. Structural failures, system reboot error logs, or the collision of unintended material – these all lead to the discovery of the new fabric that is the surface of experimental architecture.

While the architectural fabric [of Orange County] is currently "smooth" by the creation and acceptance of a predictable, decorative facade with a benign interior, the ability exists to create a variation in the surface that will forever create inconsistencies in the pattern. This hopes to create a new pattern itself, one where all forms of thought, idea, and exploration will be registered. Even the idea of the "Orange Curtain" as an invisible, conceptual, but nonetheless evident and incredibly powerful border between the social, political, and architectural laboratory that is Los Angeles, and its conservative, benign, and somewhat frightened adjacent neighbor becomes a potential surface. The Curtain has long served as an intellectual and cultural membrane, filtering the "unsafe" from the sanctuary of the sheltered. It thus fulfills a destiny of a virtual drawing surface, which captures the residual data left as the culture screen filters the safe from the unsafe, the neutral from the subjective. The Curtain itself becomes a most interesting point of study – as a mapping device; a translation machine; and an artifact conversion filter.

This record attempts to locate my work as a geological map of Orange County within the confines of its self-imposed architectural deception. It also begins to use the adjacency of the two powerful yet different counties as a binary filter in which to map the projects, which have been subdivided into three classifications: The EConomi[cal], The GRaphi[cal], and The THeoreti[cal]. This "core sampling" will survey sample projects from each of the 3 strata, and will further continue to partition the work by project typologies within the categories.

In the case of the road repair, these illustrations can be made in multidimensions: road surfaces, fissures, and patches. The road surface – the base plane, the physicality of the OC, by a brief survey of EConomi[cal] projects – either built or proposed – establishes the foundation of the application or operating system. The documents that are produced from a meshing of operating system and software application. The fissures and ruptures in the surface act as an initial GRaphi[cal] stratum. They are a method of overlays that attempt to reposition the built work and serve as a hinge to the rhetoric of the theory layer. They are considered to be an *augmented reality* interface that mediates the two adjacent layers. The nature of a text is this, in essence, as the page surface acts as an augmented or modified viewport to the suggestive or representational qualities of images within a 2D library. It is my hope that the viewing of said augmentation gives each observer the opportunity to [mis]understand the work, and therefore extract a sliver from the vibration of ExperiMental Architecture. This is an essential layer, as the entire book suggests a functionality of a *Milgram's Reality-Virtuality Continuum*, encompassing all possible variations and compositions of real **[EC]** and *virtual* / theoretical **[TH]** objects. This layer also behaves similar to the mirror in *Through The Looking Glass* – the membrane of transformation and translation between two different but closely adjacent worlds.

The errant asphalt patches begin to speak of the nature of the THeoreti[cal] layer. The places in which the path is no longer followed, the initial problem no longer solely addressed, at least in traditional terms. They reflect directly the graphic zone below, and are tempered by the shadow of the layers below.

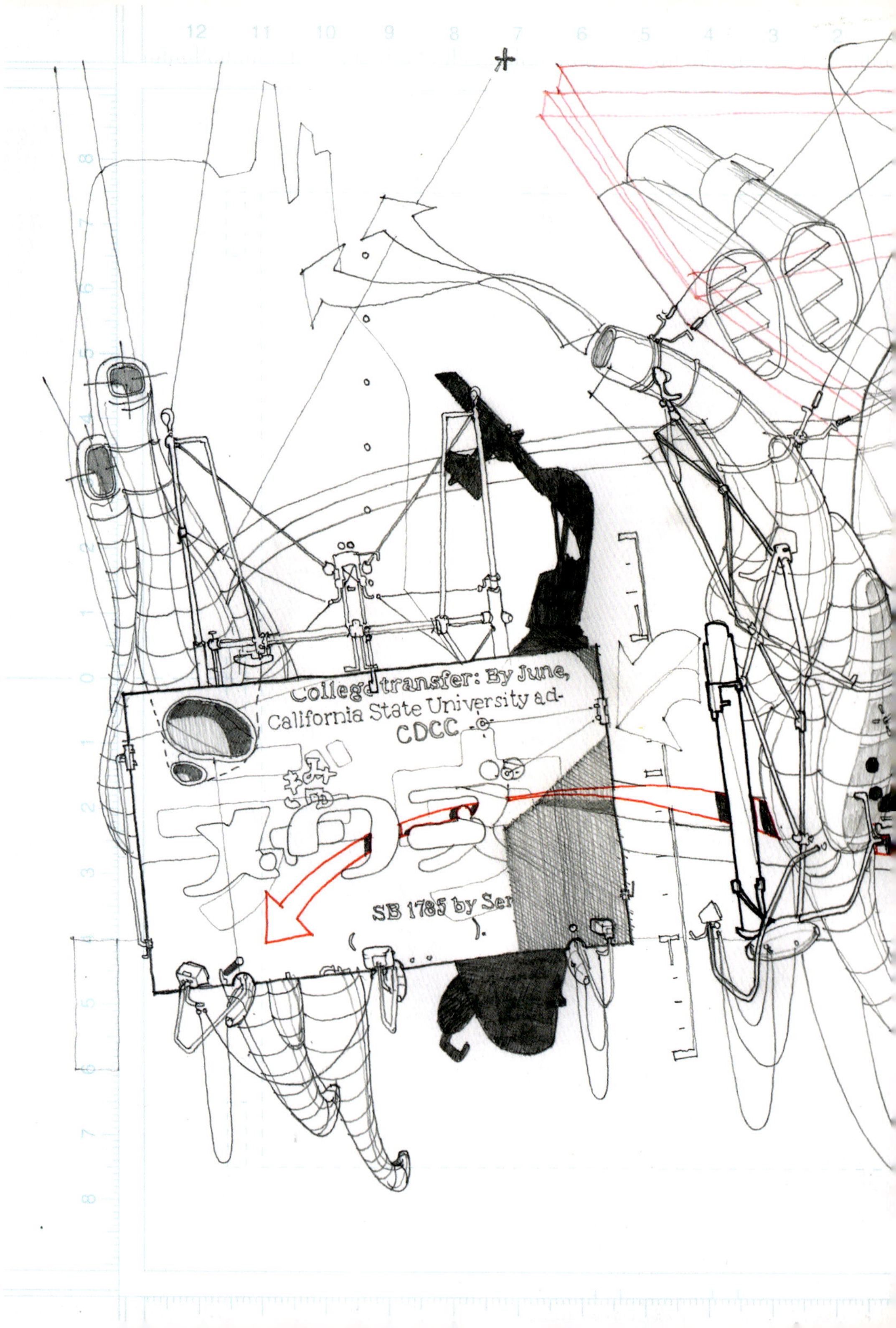
College transfer: By June,
California State University ad-
CDCC
SB 1785 by Ser
).

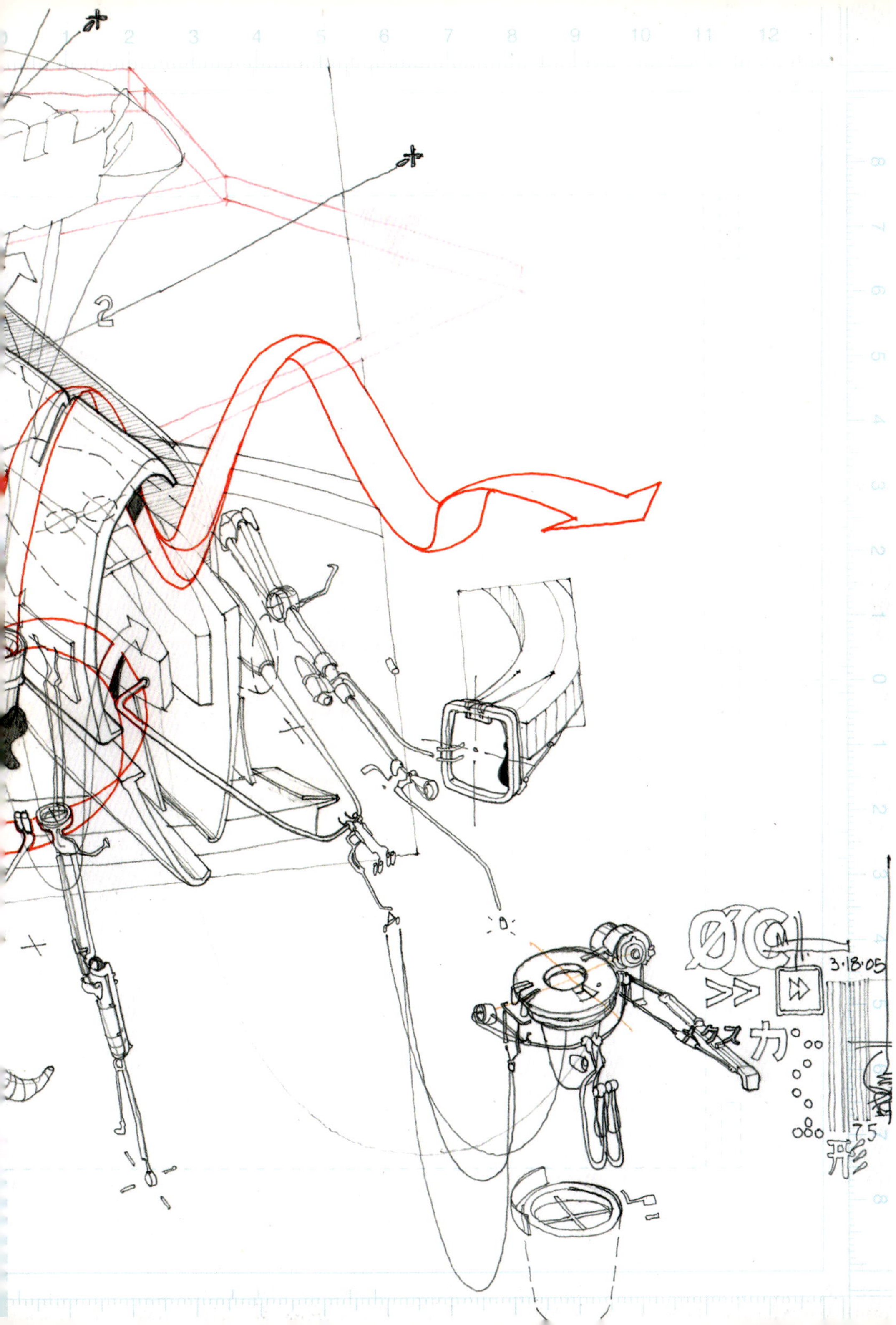
2
ØC
3·18·05
カ
7.5
形

ムならそへすたる モせた

DIGITAL PAPERSHIFT
11.15.02

Biography

Bryan W. Cantley / [Form:uLA Dimension Laboratory] 2011

Professor of Design Theory/Architecture
CSUF, SCI-ARC, Woodbury University

Form:uLA is a design practice, currently located in the Los Angeles area, owned by Bryan Cantley.
Cantley attempts to blur the undefined zone between art and architecture, considering space and its representation to be the true medium of the architect.

A set of five models and six drawings were purchased by the **San Francisco Museum of Modern Art** as a part of their permanent collection of Architecture, Design, and Digital Arts in 2001. Other exhibits of note include a featured exhibition at the Form Zero Bookstore/Gallery in Los Angeles; and solo exhibitions *"Enantiomorph Inversion Factor"* at the Architecture Gallery at Cal Poly Pomona and *"Wool and H20"* at the **UCLA** School of Architecture.

Cantley has lectured at a number of architecture schools internationally, and was featured in **SF MoMA's** "Perfect Acts of Architecture" lecture series. He additionally lectured at the **Los Angeles Forum for Architecture and Urban Design** as part of their "Out There Doing IT" lecture series. He has also served as visiting faculty at SCI-ARC and Woodbury Universities for architecture theory – where his students have captured "best thesis" project awards at both institutions. Form:uLA conducted a graduate architectural drawing seminar at The Bartlett in 2008.

He was invited to join the prestigious **Drawing Center**'s Viewing Program in New York in 2006. Form:uLA installed a solo exhibition and was an International Guest Lecturer at the **Bartlett School of Architecture** in London in October of 2008.

Cantley was the recipient of a **Graham Foundation Grant** in 2002.

His work has been featured in **Developing Digital Architecture**, Digital Architecture, Hybrid Drawings, Axonometric Drawing, and Composite Drawing. In addition, his work has appeared in magazines such as *Ray Gun*, ***Loudpaper, LA Architect,*** and "Drawing Strength from Machinery" was published in **AD** in 2008.

Form:uLA has shown work in a number of group exhibitions. From November 2001 to February 2002 they were part of a group show at **SF MoMA** entitled *Organic/Inorganic: Selections from the Permanent Collection of Architecture and Design at the San Francisco Museum of Modern Art*. At the same time, the studio also held a solo show – *Information Retrieval* – at the 3A Garage Gallery in San Francisco. Form:uLA participated in the *New Blood 101 Millennium Models* exhibition at the Pacific Design Center in Los Angeles as part of West Week 2000.

education:
1990 Master of Architecture, UCLA.
1996 Doctoral Equivalent in Visual Arts from California State University Fullerton.
1987 BA in Architecture, University of North Carolina @ Charlotte.

Full Professor, Design Theory – California State University Fullerton.

Project Credits

Temple of Laughter
Design Team: Bryan Cantley + Kevin O'Donnell — Photography: Gene Ogami, Chris Wormald

Mobile Gatherspace — Design: Bryan Cantley — Digital Model: Drew Partridge
Renderings: Rob Mothershed + Form:uLA — Photography: Gene Ogami, Chris Wormald

Placemaker/Seedplanter — Design: Bryan Cantley — Photography: Gene Ogami, Form:uLA

The Batman Series
San Francisco Museum of Modern Art, Accessions Committee Fund purchase
© Form:uLA Dimension Laboratory. — Design Team: Bryan Cantley + Kevin O'Donnell
Photography: Ian Reeves, Form:uLA

i-P.O.D. — Design Team: Bryan Cantley + Kevin O'Donnell + Ray Varela — Digital Models: Jason Allen
Client: Carrier Johnson Architects

Enantiomorphistic Inversions – Through the Looking-Glass Housing [The Alice Projects]
Design Team: Bryan Cantley + Kevin O'Donnell — Photography: Chris Wormald

Threshold/Knock Knock — Design: Bryan Cantley — Photography: Gene Ogami

Wallmaker — Design: Bryan Cantley — Photography: Form:uLA + Chris Wormald

3A Models — Design Team: Bryan Cantley + Kevin O'Donnell — Photography: Form:uLA + Gene Ogami
Drawings: Form:uLA — Client: Mark Horton 3A Gallery

Housing Prototype NH02 — Design: Bryan Cantley — Renderings: Bryan Cantley + Rob Mothershed

X.Com — Design Team: Bryan Cantley + Kevin O'Donnell + Kim Quon
Photography: Form:uLA + Jan Bruins

TnA [Truth and Advertising]
Design Team: Bryan Cantley + Kevin O'Donnell, Courtney Linker — Architect of Record: Nester & Gaffney
Renderings: Bryan Cantley + Rob Mothershed — Photography: Form:uLA — Client: Truth and Advertising

San Clemente CON-do RE:*surf*Face
Design Team: Bryan Cantley + Cameron Crockett — Renderings: Bryan Cantley

Santa Ana Monument Sign
Design: Bryan Cantley — Renderings: Rob Mothershed + Bryan Cantley
Client: Truth and Advertising / City of Santa Ana

Book Team:
Dr. Dora Epstein-Jones, Co-Author
Andrea Lopez, Editorial Research

Acknowledgments

To Talia – The best work I ever produced. You challenge me on a daily basis to keep it real.

To Kevin – My [design] partner in crime for 15 years. You helped me craft that *"Form:uLA sound."* We believed when no one else did. My deepest gratitude, my sincere respect, and my friendship. Knave?

And especially to Kim, my love – you are the one. Thank you for helping me keep it together, for your love and support. If not for you, this book literally would not be.

To Mom and Dad – where do I start?

Dora – a MOST extraordinary job. You rock.

Thanks to RIEA [Guy Lafranchi, Corrado Curti, H1, Donatella, and Marcia] for this wonderful opportunity. Aaron, Neil, and Wes for your brilliant essays [and making me look good]; CSUF School of the Arts [esp. Jerry Samuelson]; Michael Gallis, Deb Ryan, and Nelson Benzing [UNCC]; Rob Mothershed; Drew Partridge + all the great interns; Ben Refuerzo, Eugene Kupper, Doug MaCleod [UCLA]; Cameron Crockett and Ray Varela – for helping me lift the curtain; Martin Smekal and Tablet Kiosk; The Graham Foundation; Fujitsu; SFMOMA; Raybro Inc. [S&S]; Joe Biel, for the insightful dialogue; Andrea Lopez, an organizational tour de force; Rebecca Zerbst, Joe Duffy, and the few clients that trusted our vision enough to allow us to build; to my students; and to the vast Internet following I have enjoyed over the years – thank you for your support of the work!

"I'm thankful for my Daddy cause he draws pictures for me
when I can't draw them by myself and he draws the rest."
Talia, 2001